CONTENTS

ACKNOWLEDGEMENTS

Many people have generously contributed their time, experience and expertise to help with the preparation of this book. Particular thanks go to:

Jonathan Armstead, bluestone design
Helen Butt, Labrys Multimedia
Chris Craddock, Creative Link
Lucy Gledhill
Rosie and Dennis Palmer
Eileen Driscoll, Don Speake and Co.
Ian Loseby, Arris
Jonothon Potter
Sally Smith
Conrad Stead
Helen Woodcock

INTRODUCTION

'I'm a designer.' Sounds great, doesn't it? The title conjures up an immediate image of somebody who is fashionable, young, familiar with contemporary culture, creative, maybe slightly off the wall... Somebody who has a career that allows them to give full rein to their imagination... Somebody cutting-edge...

There are elements of truth in that description – but there's also more than a little fiction. This book will help you to consider what a career in the design industry will really be like, and to differentiate between spin and real life.

WHAT'S THIS BOOK ABOUT?

Google 'careers+advice+design' and you'll come up with in excess of 698,000 hits. There is so much information available on the Internet about careers in design that you may wonder if a book like this serves any real purpose. Surely you can find out what you want to know yourself?

The problem is too much information. It will take you a long time to wade through the many thousands of websites that are on offer. You may find yourself distracted by irrelevancies – or limiting the scope of your search and not finding out what you really need to know.

This book serves a number of purposes.

- It introduces some of the many careers in design that you might want to consider. Each chapter looks at a particular area and gives general information about what the field involves, relevant professional and educational qualifications and ways to get started on your career.

■ In preparing the book, we've talked to practitioners to get an inside view of the various career areas – warts and all. This will give you a more rounded impression of what working life may be like than the publicity material you'll find on education and professional organisations' websites.

■ There are addresses and web links to further sources of information so that you can carry out your own, more detailed research.

You'll meet a number of designers in this book who describe their careers. Hopefully their advice will prove both useful and stimulating. It's worth remembering, however, that the design industry is a fluid and ever-changing environment that doesn't have a set of 'career rules'. Don't be surprised or concerned if your career path is not the same as the ones you read about here. Successful designers haven't always followed a conventional path to get to where they are today. Unlike accountancy, teaching or the law, this isn't an industry where there is an automatic progression through education into the profession. Neither do designers always follow a structured career path; many have served an 'apprenticeship' as junior designers with an organisation before going on to set up their own businesses, or they've moved with some rapidity from organisation to organisation. You will find your own way into the industry through a combination of talent, skills, persistence and luck. What we are giving you are some starting points to help you design your own future.

Finally, because it's a book, *Design Uncovered* is small, so it's fully portable and you can glance at sections of it whenever you have a few spare moments. Surfing the Web is a great way to find out all you need to know – but it's not always convenient if you're sitting on the Tube or lying in the bath!

Treat this book as your starting point for a bright new career, and enjoy!

Chapter One
WHAT IS DESIGN?

LET'S START AT THE BEGINNING...

'Design' is one of those words that we use a lot without examining its real meaning. In the context of this book, we're talking about a creative process that produces an end result: innovative products, beautiful rooms, eye-catching graphics, exciting new fashions, etc.

Note those two words, 'creative' and 'process'. They are key to the success of any designer. You can't be a designer unless you have some degree of creative talent and the ability to 'see' in a way that positively impacts on other people. Neither can you be a successful designer unless you have the discipline to work through the design process, to draft your ideas over and over again, and to meet strict constraints imposed by the people who'll use your designs.

IS DESIGN THE CAREER FOR YOU?

On the following page is a multiple-choice question. Answer honestly and tick all the answers that apply to you.

You're thinking of a career in design because:

☐ a you've always liked drawing things.

☐ b you met someone in a pub who said he was a designer, drove an Audi convertible, made more than £100,000 a year and never went into his office before noon.

☐ c you helped your friend redecorate her house and she thought your ideas were really, really good.

☐ d you want to be a 'creative'.

☐ e none of the above.

Hopefully your response was 'e'. If it was any of the other options, you're likely to struggle to earn a living and be very disappointed by the work.

Don't get the wrong idea. A career in design can be rewarding, exciting and varied. It can introduce you to stimulating people, and give you plenty of opportunities to express your ideas to a large audience. Most of the designers who contributed to this book wouldn't trade their careers for anything but a Lottery rollover win. But one point they were all eager to make was that design as a career choice involves hard work and a firm grasp of business principles. It's not a pastime for dilettantes.

There are thousands of designers working in the UK. Some work alone, others are employed by large corporations. Some *are* earning in excess of £100,000; others are barely making ends meet. Some design products; others design work processes. Some wear Paul Smith suits when they go to their open-plan, city-centre offices; others wear their pyjamas and work on the kitchen table. This is an industry that is full of variety and contradictions.

The important word in that last sentence is 'industry'. Design is a business process with a specific purpose.

It's important to be realistic about what a career in design involves because this is a very competitive field in which to work. An awful lot of people think they'd like to be designers but only a few genuinely succeed in making a good living from it. Ironically, the explosion in the number of design courses offered by higher education institutions is contributing to the problem. There are more graduates than jobs, and it's harder than ever to get that all-important first break.

If these words of caution haven't put you off, then you're already on the right track because you have obviously thought realistically about why you think this is the career choice for you.

Let's try that multiple choice again. Tick all the answers that apply to you.

> The real purpose of design – and that includes engineering design and architecture – is to get someone to do something, to create an action or a reaction from an audience. It's not about your preferences, but about appealing to others. If you love colours and want to express yourself, then go into commercial or fine art.
>
> (Ian Loseby, Arris)

You're thinking of a career in design because:
- ☐ a you have a genuine passion for innovation and for coming up with new ways of looking at the world.
- ☐ b you have a good eye for colour, shape and scale.
- ☐ c you already show talent for art and design, and have started building a portfolio for your own pleasure.
- ☐ d you enjoy using computer software.
- ☐ e you understand that good design can make the difference between a product or service succeeding or failing.

Hopefully you ticked all of them! If so, you're ready to start investigating careers in design and finding out just what's involved.

SO WHAT *IS* DESIGN?

In January 2009, Royal Mail launched a series of ten stamps featuring classic British designs of the twentieth century. The set included pictures of:

- the Supermarine Spitfire, the Battle of Britain fighter aircraft designed by R.J. Mitchell

- the miniskirt, designed by Mary Quant in the 1960s

- the Mini car, designed by Sir Alec Issigonis, which became both a fashion statement and a means of transport

- the anglepoise lamp, designed by George Carwardine, the first desk lamp that really did its job

- Concorde, the supersonic jet capable of twice the speed of sound, designed by Aerospatiale and BAC

- the K2 telephone kiosk, the bright-red and glass telephone box designed by Sir Giles Gilbert Scott

- the polypropylene chair, designed by Robin Day and used in public buildings throughout the world

- Penguin Books classic book jacket design by Edward Young

- the London Underground map that Harry Beck designed, based on an electrical wiring diagram

- the Routemaster bus designed by Douglas Scott and Colin Curtis, which became a symbol of London.

These stamps highlight different areas of design – vehicles and aircraft, fashion, products, furniture and graphics – in which British designers have excelled. This country has always had a reputation for innovation, and throughout history our designs have served as prototypes for style trends that have flourished across the world.

Launching the stamps for Royal Mail, Mary Quant said: 'I am highly honoured that the banana split dress with a mini skirt has been included in the Royal Mail Design Classics issue and to be amongst such great company. Britain has the best art and design schools in the world and this attracts students from around the globe. The stamps are absolute design classics.'

What makes these designs iconic is the way that they combine style with function. The articles are good to look at – and they serve a practical purpose. They are aesthetically pleasing and easy to use. Arguably, that is the secret of good design.

Ultimately, design is about problem-solving. The design process begins when a problem or need is identified. Then the designers work through a structured sequence in which they research information and explore ideas until they come up with a potential solution.

What design isn't about is supporting your own ego. It's about helping your clients to achieve something they need to achieve, not about you coming up with brilliant ideas that will make you world-famous – or about buying that Paul Smith suit.

Of course, not everyone agrees with this definition. Many designers and pundits seek to elevate design to an art form.

In 2004, there was a major row at London's Design Museum when Chairman James Dyson – designer of the famous 'cyclonic' vacuum cleaner – resigned because of the museum's change in direction. He believed that Museum Director Alice Rawsthorn had betrayed the museum's mission to 'encourage serious design of the manufactured object'. Dyson thinks that design is 'how something works, not how it

> Design has been defined as the process that links creativity and innovation. It does this by shaping ideas to become practical and attractive propositions for users or customers. Innovation – the successful exploitation of ideas – requires the use of design to develop new products, services or processes. This interdependency is why design is now increasingly seen as a vital part of innovation along with business and technological expertise.
>
> (Source: Design Council Briefing 01 – 'The impact of design on business')

looks – the design should evolve from the function'. His vacuum cleaners are iconic examples of modern product design – but essentially they suck up dirt. Rawsthorn's agenda was somewhat different and her exhibition programme included Manolo Blahnik shoes, typography from *Harper's Bazaar* and the work of 1950s flower arranger Constance Spry. Dyson believed that she was elevating style at the expense of substance.

What this row did was to show how divided the design world is about its role and function. So the answer to the question 'What is design?' is up to the individual. In this book, we're looking at it from a business point of view because we want to help would-be designers start their careers – and to do that they have to be realistic about what the work involves.

The designers we interviewed for this book made the same point over and over again: design is a complex mix of creativity, communication and business skills. As Jonathan Armstead, who runs creative branding solutions agency bluestone design, says: 'Design is a funny industry. Obviously the creative part is paramount – but it's also about producing solutions that are functional and affordable. You can't afford to be precious about your ideas. You have to listen to clients – and ultimately what determines everything is cost.'

His thoughts are echoed by Ian Loseby, from branding agency Arris:

> To be a designer, you have to be a problem-solver – design is a problem-solving discipline rather than a decorative process. I enjoy solving other people's problems, seeing things from a different perspective, thinking differently and getting the response that everybody is looking for. I think my main driver is seeing clients happy because their problem has been solved or they've done well out of the design solution.

What they – and many others – are saying is that successful designers have their feet firmly on the ground. They understand the basic business principles that drive their clients' organisations, they can balance a budget and they can communicate their ideas convincingly.

BIG BUSINESS?

Although the term 'design' is often used generically, the industry itself covers many different areas. The Design Council identifies six major disciplines.

1   Communications design (graphics, brand, print, information design, corporate identity)

2   Product and industrial design (consumer/household products, furniture, industrial design (including automotive design, engineering design, medical products))

3   Interior and exhibition design (retail design, office planning/workplace design, lighting, display systems, exhibition design)

4   Fashion and textiles design

5   Digital and multimedia design (website, animation, film and television idents, digital design, interaction design)

6   Other (a term used to cover advertising, aerospace design, building design, landscape design, jewellery design, mechanical design, etc.).

The Design Council has compiled a bank of facts and figures about the design industry. As with all statistics, they are pretty much out of date before they are published but they do give a useful insight into the scale of the design industry and its demographic.

■   185,500 people work in design in the UK. That figure includes 'non-creatives' such as managers and administrators.

■   The turnover of UK design businesses totalled £11.6 billion in 2004–05. This sum is spread across a lot of companies: 77% of design businesses have a turnover of less than £100,000 a year.

■   More than half of all UK design businesses work in communications, digital and multimedia design.

- Traditionally this is an industry that provides scope for freelancers and small groups of associates: there are 47,400 freelance and self-employed designers and 59% of design consultancies employ fewer than five people.

At the time of the last analysis (Labour Force Survey 2003–04) the design industry was still conforming to the stereotype of being dominated by young white men in the south-east of England.

- 62% of designers are under 40.

- 61% of designers are men.

- 6% of designers are from minority ethnic groups.

- 31% of design businesses are based in London; 40% of the larger businesses employing more than 250 staff are based in London.

(All statistics taken from the Design Council, Design Industry Research www.designcouncil.org.uk)

Although statistics need to be treated with caution, there are some facts that emerge that may impact on your career.

- Certain areas of design are a good career choice for people who like working either alone or in small organisations. Nine out of ten design consultancies in interior and exhibition design, and in digital and multimedia design, have fewer than five employees.

- Although the design industry is concentrated in London and the south of England, designers themselves can work almost anywhere. You'll find small businesses and consultancies in almost every town across the UK – and a lot of freelancers working in isolated locations, from Land's End to John O'Groats, and overseas. As long as you have good communication links and are willing to work 'down the wire', you can maintain contact with your clients and stay in business.

- Designers have opportunities to diversify. Many consultancies and freelancers work across more than one discipline. According to the Design Council, 50% of all businesses working in communications also work in digital and multimedia design. Although this can be demanding – as a practitioner you'll have to work hard to keep abreast of changes in consumer preferences and technology – it means that you can adapt your skills and run less risk of them becoming obsolete. So, for example, many traditional book designers and illustrators have moved into website design and production.

■ The public is design aware. When we buy something, we're as likely to judge it on its aesthetic appeal as its durability. Whether it's fashion, interiors, mobile phones, or cars, we want them to look good. That means there is a constant demand for design services. Obviously no industry is recession-proof, but the services of a talented designer with a firm grasp of business principles will always be in demand.

Jonathan Armstead thinks that an economic downturn isn't a bad thing for the design industry: 'Companies will continue to invest in design because they recognise the need to make more noise, and that they have to do more to promote their unique qualities. That's an opportunity for companies like ours to move forward.'

THE DESIGN COUNCIL

Your first port of call to find out about different design sectors and disciplines should be the Design Council website. It's packed with useful, up-to-date information that provides a great introduction to the industry (www. designcouncil.org.uk).

Established more than 60 years ago, the government-funded Design Council is the national strategic body for design.

The website is a mine of information. It includes a series of papers on topics including how to write a design brief, ergonomics, computer-aided design,

We believe design can help people to do what they do, better... we promote the use of design throughout the UK's businesses and public services. We demonstrate that design can play a vital role in strengthening our economy and improving our society.

(Source: www.designcouncil. org.uk)

materials, trends and market research. The 'Live Issues' section has essays from industry movers and shakers on topical subjects, and its case studies examine the influence of design on business success and our lifestyles in general.

There is also a section on the site that features designers talking about their work and outlining their working routines – invaluable if you want to get a flavour of different disciplines.

Part of the Design Council's remit is to carry out research on the impact of design. *The Value of Design Factfinder* contains research from the *Design Council National Survey of Firms 2005 and Added Value Research 2007*. It is worth examining because it offers some valuable information about the way that businesses view design and purchase their design services. Their research indicates:

- a positive relationship between valuing design and growing a business: businesses that place less importance on design only grew moderately, stayed the same size or shrank in size

- just over half of the UK's businesses use designers, with one in five commissioning external agencies. However, employing designers internally is the preferred method

- personal recommendation is the most popular way for businesses to find and choose a designer

- nine out of ten businesses buy all their design from within the UK, and don't shop for services abroad. The same proportion is satisfied with the services that they buy.

Don't dismiss these statistics as irrelevant to you. They give a snapshot of the industry and suggest which disciplines are likely to increase in demand for creative, qualified and experienced designers.

A FEW WORDS ABOUT MONEY...

We've deliberately avoided including specific salary information in this book because it's hard to find any information that is valid in the long term. The amount that designers earn varies wildly depending on:

- what discipline they work in

- whether they work for a large or small organisation

- where they work (salaries are higher in London and the south-east)

- the state of the economy.

However, we accept that anyone considering a new career is interested in salary, so here is some *very general* financial information.

Salaries are not brilliant, particularly when you start out as a designer. There is a lot of competition for jobs, and this is a creative industry where people are expected to work for love rather than money. If you become a partner or director of a successful agency then you could be raking in the dosh – but it's unlikely, particularly in the current economic climate.

- Junior designers can expect a salary of between £13,000 and £20,000, depending on where they work. Many young designers have to subsidise their salaries when they start out. Competition for first jobs is such that some agencies report young graduates offering to work for free for a few months so they can get work experience.

- Middle-ranking designers with two to three years' experience can anticipate salaries in the region of £22,000 to £28,000.

- Senior designers could hope to be earning £40,000 to £60,000.

- At partner or director level, your earnings will relate to the company's profits, so the sky is the limit – or you could be counting the pennies.

This information is very, very general. Organisations that employ designers vary enormously so there are no rules. If you go to work for a large company that has an in-house product design department, you may have a formal salary structure, pension plan, private health insurance, on-site gym and health club, and all the perks of life in a corporate environment. If you work for a small agency (as many designers do), your boss may treat you all to a drink on Friday night to thank you for your hard work – and that will be the full extent of your 'perks'.

In the next chapter we'll look in more detail at the different fields of design that this book covers and what factors you should consider when you're choosing an area in which to specialise. Meanwhile, here are a couple of suggestions for things that you can do to broaden your knowledge of the design field.

◉ Take action

- Think carefully about whether you have the dedication and persistence, as well as the creative talent, to carve out a career for yourself in design. We suggest that you talk to qualified people who can advise you about your career choices, such as school, college or university careers advisors.

- Think about how your career ambitions marry up with your personal commitments. Will you be able to go where the jobs are? Can you deal (both financially and emotionally) with job insecurity and the fact that it may take a long time before you earn a decent salary?

- Start your own research. Use the Internet (though, as we've already said, this can be frustrating because there's so much information out there and a lot of it is irrelevant) and libraries to find out about current trends in design. Get copies of some of the main design magazines, such as *Design Week*, *Wallpaper* or *Icon*, and look at the areas they focus on.

- If you're seriously considering a career in design, make every effort to visit the Design Museum in London. Twenty-five years ago, Terence Conran established the forerunner of the Design Museum, the Boilerhouse, in the basement of the Victoria & Albert Museum. The Design Museum is now one of the world's leading museums devoted to contemporary design in every form, from furniture to graphics, and architecture to industrial design. Its permanent collection includes over 1,000 pieces of contemporary and twentieth-century design, including selections of domestic artefacts such as radios, computers, typewriters and chairs. Depending on what is on show at any particular time, you could see highlights from the collection such as Clive Sinclair's electric vehicle, the C5, the Hot Berta Kettle designed by Philippe Starck, and the recently acquired ambitious One Laptop Per Child by Yves Behar.

Chapter Two
CHOOSING YOUR FIELD

In this chapter, we give a brief introduction to the different design fields that are covered in *Design Uncovered*. You'll find more detailed information in subsequent chapters.

The term 'design' covers a wide range of different areas. We focus on seven specific disciplines, but it's important to recognise that the distinctions between them are often blurred. Graphic designers may be involved in brand design; textile designers may also be product designers; interior designers may also be exhibition designers; and interactive media designers are everywhere. As you read this book you'll meet some of the designers more than once; that's because they work across more than one design discipline.

At a corporate level, large organisations are recognising that an interdisciplinary approach to design brings major benefits.

Role of design

Isolating design as a single factor in business success is problematic. It can ignore the relationship between use of design and factors such as company size, sector and culture. It can also play down the contribution of other factors such as strategy, marketing and sales, which can themselves incorporate design to an extent that goes unreported...

The Department for Innovation, Universities and Skills (DIUS) has recently demonstrated that design is a core capability that shapes open innovation practice, and that design is given higher importance by firms which have such practices. Design Council research has found the design function being used by global companies to foster innovation across organisational boundaries.

- LEGO has developed a new design system to run its whole innovation process. The programme aligns corporate objectives and design strategy, and puts designers at the heart of multidisciplinary project teams. The system has allowed LEGO to cut its average design cycle from two years to six months.

- Virgin Atlantic Airways uses design as a key competitive differentiator. It locates designers across the business to allow for cross-functional sharing of ideas; and has created a service design department which works with the crew management and HR departments to develop and deliver new offerings.

(Source: Design Council Briefing 01 – 'The impact of design on business')

We've divided the different types of design careers according to the model used by the Chartered Society of Designers, where every member is allocated a Design Discipline Group, reflecting the discipline in which they were assessed and in which they are recognised as competent by the Society.

WHAT IS PRODUCT DESIGN?

'Product design' is a broad term that covers a range of functions including: engineering-based, three-dimensional products; environmental and interactive information technology design; transportation and automotive design; furniture and craft-related products, such as ceramics, glass, jewellery, silver and leather goods.

Product designers work closely with other people in developing new products of every type, from paperclips to aircraft. They may come up with ideas, but these ideas have to work in practice – so they have to fit in with a wider development process. If a business decides it wants to produce a new widget, that widget has to:

■ meet the needs of the target market, i.e. the widget users

■ be technically feasible

■ meet production parameters – for example, its costs must fit in with company budgets.

You could create the best-looking widget in the world but if the manufacturer can't afford to produce it in sufficient numbers at a price that consumers will tolerate, that widget is useless.

Product designers must therefore work closely with product developers – who may range from scientists to technicians to professional researchers and marketing specialists. Depending on the type of product they are designing they may need a lot of technical knowledge. Obvious examples are vehicle and aviation designers, who will need to know what factors influence the shape of cars and aircraft. Equally, someone who designs bathroom tiles will need to understand the manufacturing process and the science of ceramics.

Many designers in this discipline work for large companies and follow a structured career path: after graduation, they get an internship or graduate traineeship that gives them experience across their organisation; then they move into a particular area of design. Of all types of designers, these are most likely to experience corporate culture – with all its bonuses and drawbacks.

WHAT IS EXHIBITION DESIGN?

Every year thousands of exhibitions are staged across the country. Some of these feature permanent displays and some only last for a few days.

Like interior design, exhibition design involves creating an environment that people can walk through – so designers must work in three dimensions.

Permanent exhibitions are built to last for a long time and are a common feature in the heritage industry; museums, stately homes and art galleries will house permanent exhibitions of the artefacts that they own and want to put on continual display. Similarly, many large organisations will stage permanent exhibitions to display their work to visitors and to show how their business has developed since its inception.

Temporary exhibition design is about the creation of a non-permanent environment that communicates with an audience. Temporary displays may be used to promote a brand, for example at a major international business or commercial exhibition, or they might be set up by a college to display information about its achievements. Designing temporary exhibitions demands a particular set of skills because you're usually working within very strict parameters of space and materials, and whatever you construct must be easily erected and taken down when required.

Exhibition designers need a range of skills, particularly the ability to think in three dimensions, and to combine creativity with technical knowledge about construction methods and materials.

WHAT IS FASHION AND TEXTILE DESIGN?

Designers who work in fashion and textiles do more than come up with ideas for new clothes. They design garments, bags, footwear, millinery and other accessories; patterns for surfaces including printed textiles and carpets, papers, ceramics and tiles; woven and knitted textiles including non-printed wall coverings and laminates.

According to the *Clothing and Footwear Industry Market Review*, the UK market for these products was worth an estimated £48.55 billion in 2007. This accounted for only 6% of total consumer spending, an all-time low. However, this isn't because we're buying fewer clothes and shoes; it's because the cost of these articles is much lower than it has ever been. The interest in – and demand for – fashion products remains as high as ever. That means there is still scope for successful careers in fashion and textile design.

Fashion designers mainly work in one of the following fields.

- High-street fashion, where garments are mass-produced and sold in dedicated clothes stores such as Next or supermarkets such as George at Asda – new clothes ranges are introduced every few weeks so there is constant demand for new products.

- Ready-to-wear – middle-weight designers like Maxmara produce ready-to-wear clothes, usually in fairly small numbers that are sold through shops and catalogues.

- Haute couture – one-off garments that are produced for special collections or to meet a client's specific order.

Another area in which they work is costume design, where they design, create and source costumes and accessories for television, film and theatre productions.

Textile designers create two-dimensional designs that are used in commercial or artistic fabrics or textile products. The two main areas in which they work are textiles for clothing (either for fashion clothes or specialist items like uniforms or protective clothing), and textiles for soft furnishings (upholstery, curtains, etc.) and bed linen.

They may also produce designs for paper goods such as wrapping paper, packaging and greetings cards.

Achieving success in this field is not easy – it's highly competitive and the openings are limited. One characteristic that tends to distinguish fashion and textile designers is their determination to succeed – even if that means working long hours for meagre financial rewards until they get established. If you're thinking about this sort of career, don't kid yourself that your designs will be up there on the catwalk next to Stella McCartney's next year. If you're lucky, you may find a job as a very junior designer with a clothing manufacturer – and you'll probably need to take on another job at the same time to make ends meet.

WHAT IS GRAPHIC DESIGN?

Graphic designers produce design solutions to communicate messages visually. Their work can include: type design, typography, lettering and calligraphy for reproduction; illustration; design for advertising, print and packaging; corporate identity; applied graphics for signing systems; vehicle livery and graphics on product design; architectural graphics; design for film, television or video reproduction including multi-sensual, time-based or still imagery; photography.

Graphic design underpins many other types of design. As you'll see in this book, the brand designers we talked to started life as graphic designers who produced print-based materials for their clients. Gradually their remit widened and they took on more responsibility until they were developing brands as a whole. But the starting point was graphics – the visual messages that are communicated through print and images, layout and colour.

This is a popular field that offers numerous opportunities for diversification. However, you have to have creative talent and an eye for detail if you're going to succeed. Computer technology has opened up the field of graphic design to the masses; everyone from your six-year-old nephew to your 60-year-old grannie can knock up a leaflet on their PC. But few people can develop a design that really works in that it catches the attention of its audience and stays in their memory for a long time afterwards.

WHAT IS INTERACTIVE MEDIA DESIGN?

Interactive media designers create an interface through which users can manipulate information technology. They work in many different areas designing websites, intranets and extranets; multimedia CD-ROMs, DVDs and kiosks; computer games; interactive elements for video DVDs, websites and mobile devices.

This is a huge growth area. Just think of the many different types of interactive media products that have been introduced to the market over the last five years, from mobile phones with Internet access to sophisticated new bank ATMs – and the public shows no sign of wearying of IT and reverting to more archaic methods of communication.

Of all the design disciplines, this is the one that offers the most employment opportunities because the thirst for high-tech is not diminishing. There is a constant demand for interactive media designers in large organisations and small agencies that specialise in a particular field.

Obviously, to succeed you're going to need a lot of technical know-how. It doesn't matter how creative you are, if you can't get to grips with the technology and master elements of programming, this isn't the discipline for you. If you have the necessary attributes, however, and you pay attention to your career path, you can look forward to an interesting and financially rewarding career.

WHAT IS INTERIOR DESIGN?

Interior design is about creating exciting, enjoyable – and practical – indoor environments. This may involve working on old buildings and adapting them for new functions, or helping to design interiors for new-builds.

Interiors may be domestic or commercial, so don't make the mistake of thinking that all interior designers are interested in is wallpaper and soft furnishings. Practitioners often specialise in a specific field such as hotel design, public spaces, offices or shops. Other areas of specialisation include industrial interiors (yes, somebody has to think about how the inside of a factory looks), and film and theatre design.

Like fashion design, there's a certain kudos attached to interior design so it's an area that attracts a lot of attention. Traditionally this has been considered a field that people have drifted into to express their artistic talents. In reality, it's a competitive discipline that demands a high degree of technical knowledge as well as creativity. Today, most interior designers follow a rigorous period of training and study with a long 'apprenticeship' in which they learn their trade and build up the contacts that will make them successful.

WHAT IS BRAND DESIGN?

Brand design involves using a number of media to create an image for a product or service that people will remember and return to. A brand designer may be involved in designing packaging, publications, point-of-sale publicity, websites, staff uniforms – anything that conveys a message about the product or service to the public.

Brands have become an increasingly important part of our lives because we now have so much choice when we want to buy something. Indeed, they're such an integral part of our lives that in some cases the names of manufacturers have become descriptors for the products themselves. 'Before I set off running this morning, I put on my Raybans, tied up my Nikes, and switched on my iPod. Then I got into my Mini, and drove to O2 so I could do a couple of laps around it. When I finished I rehydrated with some Perrier and Lucozade…' For Raybans, read sunglasses, for Nikes read running shoes, for Mini read car. As any manufacturer knows, a strong brand identity can be the key to massive financial success.

Brand design is sometimes known as 'experience' design because it focuses on the experience that a customer or consumer has with an organisation. Ideally, a brand identity will highlight the qualities that a company considers to be important, so that it sends out the right message to prospective customers. It will help to position a company so that it attracts consumers and then maintains its consumer base. So, brand design will influence the way that the product looks, is packaged, its publicity material, the way that it is merchandised and presented to the public.

Brand designers help an organisation to communicate not only its products and services, but also its culture and values to the outside world. These are presented through distinct motifs that permeate every aspect of the organisation's image. The brand designer helps the organisation to achieve consistency in the way that it presents itself.

Brand designers may work on a number of different areas of a client's business. For example, packaging plays a key role in brand perception because it can draw attention to the product and make it stand out in a crowded marketplace. A company specialising in brand design might work with product designers to create more efficient, environmentally responsible packaging that appeals to customers' 'green' instincts and thus encourages consumer loyalty. At the same time, the brand designers may also be designing logos and graphics that are used on all aspects of the company's publications, producing newsletters and catalogues, handling direct mail and advertising, and organising PR events.

For clients, it's easier (and often more cost-effective) to work with one company that takes care of every aspect of its image than to deal separately with different companies of graphic designers, interactive media designers, interior designers, etc. They can build up a close relationship with the brand designer and develop a synergistic relationship.

Increasingly, brand design is about communicating a client organisation's ethos rather than just publicising its products and services. Consumers and customers are becoming more environmentally and socially aware, and are more likely to ask questions about how an organisation operates in the widest sense. A brand designer that can communicate his or her client's caring attitude towards the environment and less advantaged communities is on to a winner. Think about the Body Shop and the way that everything about the company – from its packaging policies (bring back your bottles and get a discount) and its manufacturing processes to its shop interiors – communicates its aim to produce high-quality goods in a sustainable manner.

Designers who move successfully into this field may have started their careers as graphic designers. Crucial to their success is business acumen – you have to understand how marketing works, and how customers and consumers tick. Creativity is important for a brand designer – but highly developed business skills are equally important.

In the following chapters, you'll read more about these individual design disciplines and meet some of the people who have built up successful design careers. Hopefully this will help you to decide whether you have the skills, attitudes and dedication to follow a design career yourself.

IS DESIGN A CAREER FOR YOU?

We talked to designers from every discipline. One thing that they all agreed upon was that design is 40% creative talent and 60% hard work. It's less about thinking up 'blue-sky' visions and more about keeping an eye on the order and account books.

Graphic designer Conrad Stead lists the following skills and personal qualities as essential for a successful designer – and they apply equally to other design fields.

- An eye for design.

- To be able to listen and understand what the client wants. You have to be able to interpret a brief. Experience helps – sometimes it's what the client is *not* saying, or what they don't want, that gives you the clues.

- Willingness to keep up to date with design 'fads and fashions'. Colours, shapes, typefaces and 'feel' all change, all the time. These things date very quickly and look old-fashioned, even to an untrained eye. You need to know what's going on, what's in and what's out.

- Discipline – even if you don't work 9 to 5.30, you need to have systems in place, organisation and focus.

- Good IT skills, appropriate to your field.

WILL YOU MAKE THE GRADE?

Try the (light-hearted and non-psychometric) quiz below to see if you have the right attitude to make the grade in the creative world. Answer the questions, check the feedback, total your scores and see what we think about your chances.

 Quiz

1   You have to submit a piece of work by the end of May. It's now the second of week of April. Do you…?
- [ ] a   Wait until the week before the deadline to get started – a week is plenty of time.
- [ ] b   Start now – the more time you give yourself to prepare, the better.
- [ ] c   Forget about it until your tutor asks where it is.
- [ ] d   Do it the night before – you work better at the last minute.

2 What do you think about working in a team?
- ☐ a Great – as long as everyone follows your lead.
- ☐ c You hate it, but it's something you have to do sometimes.
- ☐ b You enjoy it – it gives you a chance to share ideas and improve the final result.
- ☐ c It's unproductive – people spend all their time talking rather than doing.

3 Your boss tells you that you'll need to work through the night to get a job finished for a client. Do you…?
- ☐ a Get on with it, but sulk – you don't get paid for overtime.
- ☐ b Refuse – there's a party tonight and no way are you missing it.
- ☐ c Agree on condition that you get extra pay or time off in lieu.
- ☐ d Accept that this is part of the job.

4 During an interview for an administrative job with an advertising agency, you're asked to sing a song. Do you…?
- ☐ a Freeze – you can't, you just can't.
- ☐ b Grit your teeth, close your eyes and sing for your life.
- ☐ c Get very excited and give them half an hour of your best karaoke numbers.
- ☐ d Ask the interviewer what they mean.

5 You're offered a one-year contract as a junior fashion designer at a very low wage. Do you…?
- ☐ a Accept – this is the break you've been waiting for.
- ☐ b Refuse – what's the point of taking a contract that will leave you out of work again in 12 months' time?
- ☐ c Accept, but tell them that you'll leave immediately if someone offers you a better deal.
- ☐ d Accept, but secretly decide to keep looking for something better.

6 Which of these statements do you identify most closely with?
- ☐ a I'm confident and not afraid to state my opinions.
- ☐ b I'm quiet, shy and hate being the centre of attention.

☐ c I'm always first up for everything – the ringleader.

☐ d I'm the coolest person I know.

7 Which of the following do you want most from your career?

☐ a Satisfaction and enjoyment.

☐ b Money.

☐ c Fame and recognition.

☐ d A quiet, well-ordered working life.

8 In a website design company, which of the following people are most important?

☐ a The designer who comes up with the concept.

☐ b The 'techies' who do the programming.

☐ c The company administrator.

☐ d Daft question – everyone in the company plays a vital role.

9 You think self-employment must be…

☐ a Great – work only when you feel like it.

☐ b Frightening – there's no job security.

☐ c Challenging – can be hard but can also be very rewarding.

☐ d For idiots – no sick pay, no paid holidays, no office to go to.

10 Your boss tells you that you have to go on a teambuilding weekend at an Outward Bound centre. Do you…?

☐ a Look forward to it – it could be fun.

☐ b Refuse – you don't do mud, rain and waterproofs.

☐ c Agree to go but decide to throw a sickie the day before.

☐ d Go but refuse to join in the activities you don't like the look of.

Feedback

Question 1

a You're cutting it too fine – you should give yourself plenty of time to redraft your ideas. *(3 points)*

b Yes – the earlier you start, the less pressure you'll be under to complete on time so you'll be able to check your work thoroughly. *(4 points)*

c   You'll either have to do the work too quickly, or not do it at all. No-brainer.
(0 points)

d   You might work faster but you won't work better. *(1 point)*

Question 2

a   You're not a team worker if you expect to be the boss all the time. *(0 points)*

b   If you resent working in a team you won't be a productive member of it.
(2 points)

c   You're a good team worker and recognise that more hands lighten the load.
(4 points)

d   You may be right sometimes – but not all teams perform badly. Give team-working a chance. *(2 points)*

Question 3

a   Not a productive attitude – who wants to work with a sulker? *(1 point)*

b   Expect to lose your job in the near future. *(0 point)*

c   You may get away with your demands but you need to show willing.
(2 points)

d   You're right – people in the media and arts rarely work regular hours.
(4 points)

Question 4

a   If a request like this makes you freeze, you may not have enough confidence
to survive in the creative and media world. *(0 points)*

b   Go for it. They're looking for your willingness to take part, not at your
performance skills. *(4 points)*

c   You may be willing – but nobody likes a showoff. *(1 point)*

d   Isn't it obvious? They want you to sing a song. *(1 point)*

Question 5

a   Good for you – it's hard to break into this type of work so you're wise to
accept the offer. *(4 points)*

b   A lot of fashion design work is short term, so you're not going to have a lot
of success with such a negative attitude. *(0 points)*

c   You're honest – but they can probably find someone else who'll be more
loyal. *(2 points)*

d   Sneaky. You're not going to make a committed member of the company.
(1 point)

Question 6

a   You'll probably do well in the design and media field. *(4 points)*

b   You may find you're uncomfortable in environments that attract outgoing
types. *(1 point)*

c   You could impress people – but you might also irritate them. Give the rest of the world a chance. *(2 points)*

d   Says who? Arrogance won't help you get ahead in the design and media field. *(1 point)*

Question 7

a   Good attitude. *(4 points)*

b   Some people make a fortune in the arts and creative fields. Most don't. *(0 points)*

c   You're likely to be dissatisfied – celebrity comes to very few people. *(0 points)*

d   You may find a niche in admin somewhere, but generally the design and creative fields are high-octane, high-energy. *(1 point)*

Question 8

a   Without technical support and admin staff, the designer wouldn't be able to deliver. *(1 point)*

b   Without designers and admin staff, the techies wouldn't have a job. *(1 point)*

c   The company administrator is part of a team of people – nobody works alone. *(1 point)*

d   You're right – all design companies are made up of teams of people, none of whom is 'most important'. *(4 points)*

Question 9

a   No – you'll work when your clients want you to, which could be 24/7. *(0 points)*

b   Depends on your type of work and how organised you are. Some self-employed people manage their careers so that they are constantly in work. *(2 points)*

c   True – you'll need to be able to accept both the highs and lows. *(4 points)*

d   If these things are important to you, you wouldn't enjoy self-employment. *(0 points)*

Question 10

a   Good attitude – make the most of the experience. *(4 points)*

b   You won't be popular – teamwork is important in creative and media fields. *(0 points)*

c   Sly – and your ruse might be spotted, so you won't win any gold stars from your boss. *(1 point)*

d   Party poopers don't get brownie points. You should try something new: it can be fun and your boss wants to know that you're a willing member of the team. *(1 point)*

✔ Check Your Score

40–30   Your answers are generally sensible and show that you
             have a realistic attitude to working in the design world.

29–20   Think seriously about your career choice – are you
             sure that this is what you really want? Remember that
             careers in design can involve long hours, and financial
             and professional insecurity.

19–10   Talk to somebody about your career choices – soon.
             You may have a very unrealistic idea about the sort of
             work you'll be doing – and that's a problem in such a
             competitive field.

10 or below We think you're reading the wrong book! Stay creative
             and keep your passions – but don't think about a
             career in design unless you're willing to change your
             attitude!

◔ Take action

- Talk to someone who works in, or is connected to,
  your chosen design field. Ask friends and family if they
  have any contacts; if you're at college or university, your
  tutors may be able to put you in contact with design
  colleagues. Ask them about their work and listen to their
  answers – don't filter out the bits you don't want to hear.

- You can read case studies and profiles of different types
  of designers on the Internet. The Design Council website
  is a good starting point. You will also find university
  course websites helpful: most of them have profiles of
  students and alumni.

Chapter Three
PRODUCT DESIGN

Everything that we use has been designed by someone. Product designers focus on the way that an article looks, feels, works, etc., so that it meets the needs of the end user. There's a more detailed explanation of this discipline in Chapter 2.

In February 2009, über-trendy magazine *Wallpaper* announced its fifth anniversary design awards: 'our annual pat on the back to the people and places that have made our year that extra bit special'.

The eclectic range of products that were celebrated give some indication of the wide influences that product designers have on every aspect of our lives. From airline accessories to floor lamps, ceramics to side tables, designers across the world are creating new products to enhance our lives both practically and aesthetically.

Product designers decide how the items that we use in our daily lives look and work. Most of them aim to make products easy to use, efficient, cost-effective to produce and good to look at. However, as with fashion, the great product designers can create pretty much anything they want to.

Product designers usually specialise in a particular area that reflects their training or experience. Some product designers know what they want to focus on before they go to college or university and look for specialist education courses, such as automotive design. Others discover their metier when they are studying and make that the focus of their work.

Because the range of products that demand design input is so great, it's hard to generalise about careers in this discipline. There are product

Furniture design, industrial design, product design, 3D design, critical design – are all part of a broader definition that is Design Products. Furniture, cameras, fly swats, telephones, clothes pegs, test tubes, cradles, cigarette lighters, fire extinguishers, knives, spoons, teapots and computers are all products of design; the fruit of some sort of a design process (be it methodical, research-led, scientific, inspirational, accidental or whatever). We will by no means attempt to narrow down or isolate a definition, for if we were to attempt to do so by saying that to design is to impose one's will on materials (extract, mould, form, assemble), what would this definition include? Or rather, is anything excluded?

(Source: www.rca.ac.uk)

designers working in huge engineering company with teams of other people, designing new tools, processes or machines; equally, there are ceramics experts working in small studios in the rural wilderness, handcrafting vases and plates.

Consequently, in this chapter we've focused on two very different areas: an industrial product designer who works for a large organisation, and a designer who specialises in handmade ceramics and is just starting out on her career.

THE IMPORTANCE OF PRODUCT DESIGN

According to Design Council research, manufacturing is the sector most positive about design in the UK. Fifty per cent of manufacturers feel design has an either integral or significant role to play in their business, compared with a UK average of 37%.

Seventy-nine per cent of manufacturers believe that design is integral to our future economic performance, and 77% recognise the link between design and profitability.

These statistics are important because these attitudes are mirrored by investment. Until the economic bloodbath of 2008–09, investment in design by manufacturers was rising significantly. There were more dedicated design departments in manufacturing businesses than there were in most other businesses, and external agencies were also getting more work from this sector than from others. This was creating a lot of new opportunities for product, digital and multimedia designers. When the recovery takes place, the manufacturing industry may be leaner but it will still need good design.

Research suggests that design is a significant source of competitive advantage for UK companies because it allows them to compete in their market on more than price. Good design that leads to the creation of innovative products and services can open up new income streams. It can stimulate exports and attract new investors. The Design Council cites two examples of this in its briefing paper, 'The impact of design on business'.

■ SmartSensor Telemed (SSt) used design to turn advanced bioscience into a user-centred home-testing kit for diabetes. It has since opened markets in the US, and the NHS is awaiting the arrival of the new kit.

■ Axon Automotive, a manufacturer of fuel-efficient cars, identified new markets for its carbon-fibre technology and designed a new brand – leading to £650,000 from the Energy Saving Trust and a Rushlight Award for innovative environmental technology in 2007.

INDUSTRIAL PRODUCT DESIGN

As one example of the importance of industrial product design, let's consider the work of automotive designers. This is a specific area of activity that is closely linked to industry: students have to merge their creative talent with a host of limiting factors that determine what our cars can do. At the same time, they have to recognise that car design is massively important to everyone who drives. Not only is our car one of the biggest purchases we make during our lifetimes, it's also frequently used as an expression of our personality. We define ourselves by giving brands of cars personalities. Most of us would accept that we expect huge differences in the character of a Porsche driver and of a Nissan Micra driver. And most of us recognise the term 'white-van man' and know to what it refers!

The industrial product design process is fairly similar, regardless of the industry. Designers will often work with researchers who have determined what the public want their products to look and feel like, and how they want them to perform. Sometimes, however, designers themselves come up with an idea that they need to sell to potential manufacturers.

A key part of product development is creating the brief. This can take a long time and the product may move through many manifestations before a final design is agreed upon.

The brief has to combine three very distinct areas.

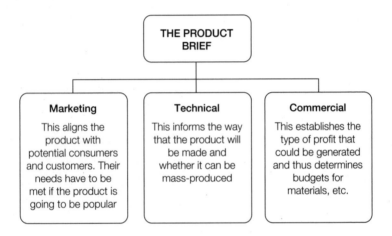

THE PRODUCT BRIEF

Marketing

This aligns the product with potential consumers and customers. Their needs have to be met if the product is going to be popular

Technical

This informs the way that the product will be made and whether it can be mass-produced

Commercial

This establishes the type of profit that could be generated and thus determines budgets for materials, etc.

Obviously these interests don't always coincide – and it may be the designer's job to come up with a solution that is acceptable to everyone.

Once the designer has taken a brief, he or she will develop ideas and prepare initial sketches, decide on appropriate materials and produce more detailed drawings using computer design software. These will be followed by samples, or working models that can be tested to see how they work, and costed to see if they meet budget restraints. Again, this can be a slow process – there may be numerous versions of the product that get through to prototype before a final version is agreed upon. Inevitably, at this stage designers will liaise closely with production managers, who influence the manufacturing process.

There may be problems that have to be ironed out in conjunction with engineers and model-makers during each phase of development. As well as designing products, designers may also take part in meetings and presentations, and put together bids and proposals for new work.

Manufacturing may take place within the company – in which case the designer can maintain a hands-on approach and help to guide the process – or be contracted overseas.

Some industrial product designers work as freelances or with small agencies that specialise in a particular type of product, but product design is a discipline in which many designers are employed by large companies.

case STUDY

I work as a design team leader within a government organisation that specialises in communications technology. I completed a degree course in electronic engineering, joined as a graduate engineer and followed a structured training programme leading to a job as a design engineer. After two years I was promoted to senior design engineer and became more involved in the management and design of specialist communication systems.

Recently I was promoted to team leader. I'm enjoying the increased managerial responsibility for planning and progressing the design of new communication systems. I estimate, plan and progress design projects and supervise designers and support staff. I also liaise with support services, co-ordinate equipment trials, meet with customers and write technical documents.

To do this job you need a comprehensive grounding in electronic engineering and design expertise. We use computer-aided design and simulation tools, so computer literacy is essential, and you have to be able to communicate ideas both verbally and in writing. Project and people management skills are important, too, because you're acting as a team leader and a team-builder.

I love the technical challenges of a project, taking a design concept from prototype to production, and I like the interaction with customers and other staff. There's a lot of variety in my work and no two days are the same. The organisation employs hundreds of graduates in a wide range of disciplines, including mechanical engineering, manufacturing, chemical engineering and materials science, and a number of them are working in design roles.

If you join on a graduate training programme, you get a development plan tailored to meet your individual needs and a series of three-month placements in different parts of the organisation. You have a mentor throughout your training to guide and advise you, and at the end of each placement there's a formal appraisal to help identify the direction your career will take.

This type of design career wouldn't appeal to everyone but I like working in a structured environment and knowing the shape that my career will take. The organisation recognises the importance of training and invests heavily to provide good development opportunities, so we have extensive training facilities.

When you complete the graduate training programme, there are opportunities to move directly into a junior management or senior technical role. You're encouraged to qualify for membership of professional institutions related to your discipline, such as IChemE, IMechE and IEE.

(Because of the nature of her work, this interviewee asked to remain anonymous.)

SMALL-SCALE CREATIVE PRODUCT DESIGN

Not every product designer works on mass-production or large-scale projects. There are thousands of individuals whose interest in art and design has led them into their own businesses producing one-off or limited edition products.

Here we profile Rosie Palmer, a ceramicist who is just embarking on her career.

Rosie Palmer's interest in contemporary crafts started at school. After A-levels, she completed a foundation course at Leeds College of Art and Design.

case STUDY

'In the first term, we worked on drawing, then went into one of four disciplines: fashion and textiles, 3D design, visual communications and fine art. I specialised in textiles, and when the course finished I started a degree course in fashion and textiles at Leeds University, but it wasn't right for me. I worked for a while and did some evening classes, then eventually went on to study contemporary crafts at University College Falmouth. You could choose the medium that you preferred and I worked a lot in ceramics – I liked the flat surfaces that you could build on, and the fact that you can do almost anything with clay before it's fired.

'We had a final show when we graduated so I got a chance to showcase my work at the Business Design Centre in London. I'd been working on a theme about bacteria and the fact that we're all overly clean – I wanted to portray friendly bacteria through a series of jugs and tiles, and I was making my products using recycled materials that connected with my theme. I sold a few pieces and it was a good opportunity to publicise what I can do. The show attracts a lot of different people – though many of them are trying to sell you something, like space on their websites through which you can market your products.

'Once you leave university, it's hard to get started. You need to keep in the loop and find out about jobs and residencies and that's difficult if you're also working to earn a living. In the long term, I'd like to make ceramics and have my own shop where I sell them and other people's products, too. Short term, I'm exploring selling through websites like Etsy and Folksy – you can have your own online shops on these websites as long as you're selling original craft items, so it's one way to get started.

'Ultimately, making a success of original product design of this type is as much about being out there and getting noticed as it is about doing the designs.'

Etsy (www.etsy.com) is an American website that provides an online marketplace for artists and crafters to sell handmade goods. Launched in 2005, by the end of 2008 it had more than 1.3 million members. When you sign up as a seller, you'll get your own online shop that you can customise with a banner and set policies for. It's an ideal sales opportunity for novice web users, since you don't need any technical know-how to get up and running. There are small fees for listing items and you pay a commission to Etsy on every sale.

Folksy champions cool crafts and design talent. We marry up designers and crafters with buyers who want individual, quality stuff that's made with love. Plus, we run design competitions and other fun stuff.

(Source: www.folksy.com)

An equivalent British website launched a couple of years ago is www.folksy.com

This also supports original craft and design talent by showcasing work and providing a cost-effective platform to sell 'stuff'. Again, you can open your own online 'shop' and pay commission on sales.

WHAT DOES IT TAKE TO SUCCEED?

If you're planning to go into product design, particularly on the industrial or manufacturing side, you'll need a range of skills. Not only do you need creative talent, you'll also need technical or engineering knowledge that is pertinent to your chosen field.

The other skills that employers value highly are those that relate to business. Manufacturers exist to make a profit; when they decide to produce something, they will look at the costs involved and the possible price at which they can sell their product. They want designers who can understand a budget and work within it, and who don't get precious about their designs.

See the diagram below for the skills you'll need to be a successful product designer.

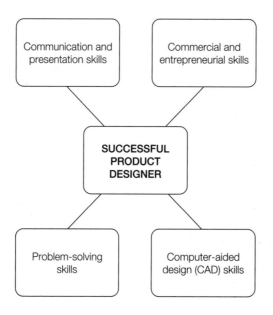

GETTING STARTED

There are various ways to get into product design, but most involve some degree of higher education. You could choose a qualification in product design, or a more general design qualification that offers product design as an option. You could also focus more on the technical and engineering aspects of design, or on specific areas, such as furniture, automotive or consumer goods.

We've included details of some different types of courses to give you an idea of the varied fields of study that are available. This is only a taster, but it will help you to appreciate the breadth of opportunities that you could access.

Aston University has no fewer than 18 product design courses, ranging from medical product design through to engineering production design. Many of these courses have a strong engineering focus and would appeal to students who have already decided that they want a technical or engineering career.

For students who want a more broad-based degree, Aston offers a BSc in Product Design and Management.

Course info

To reach the market any product must go through the essential product phase. This is central to the success of the product cycle and requires an understanding of each part of the process – market need, specification, design, manufacture, marketing, operation, distribution, maintenance and eventual disposal. This programme provides the basis of business management in addition to the underpinning Product Design modules. It will suit those designers who wish to operate across a broad range of business functions.

(Source: www.aston.ac.uk)

Course info

The evolution of existing and emergence of new technologies has profound implications for products, the people who use them and the cultures in which they are placed. This is both an exciting and daunting proposition. Innovative Product Design aims to educate hybrid designers who have the ability to evaluate and creatively use technology in a design context. Through sensitively and critically assessing the needs of people we hope our graduates can design products that have a positive impact on our changing society.

(Source: www.dundee.ac.uk)

An interesting contrast is the BSc in Product Design and Innovation at the University of Strathclyde. This combines an introduction to design with courses in marketing, business and entrepreneurship. In Year 4, students undertake an individual project in which they design a product. Recent projects include: a redesign of a nineteenth-century musical instrument, the glass armonica; a product which helps people to find items easily in their handbags; and an inclusive kitchen appliance designed to help elderly and disabled people who have impairments that prevent them from preparing meals.

Duncan of Jordanstone College of Art & Design is ranked as one of the top three art schools in the UK and offers an undergraduate BSc programme in Innovative Product Design (IPD).

The course combines elements of design with technology, commerce, people and contexts so that students get a broad appreciation of what contributes to effective product design. As well as project-based studio activity, students work closely with industry and get involved with 'live client projects' where the brief is set by industry. The aim of these projects is for students to design solutions for a real-world brief and to work directly with clients. Briefs have included working on a packaging project for a local manufacturer, and taking part in an international design challenge where Microsoft set the brief.

As with most high-profile design courses, competition for places is fierce and applicants will not only need to meet the usual academic standards for a university place, but might also be called for interview and to present a portfolio.

One of the great sources of product design training is the Royal College of Art in London (www.rca.ac.uk), the world's only postgraduate art and design school. There are 20 departments in the college, offering courses that cover the full range of design disciplines. In terms of product design, these include ceramics and glass, design products, innovation design engineering and vehicle design. Innovations such as the Ford Ka and Jaguar XK8, the PS furniture range for Ikea, Concrete Canvas – a shelter that will revolutionise disaster relief – and the Eglu chicken coop, are all the work of recent alumni. Vacuum cleaner king Sir James Dyson trained here, too.

During the two-year Design Products MA course, first- and second-year students work together in small study groups called platforms. These platforms focus strongly on the design experience and ethos.

The range and concepts are complex, so if you're interested in this field you should visit the college website and the dedicated platform websites; these will give you a much clearer idea of the type of work students are involved in.

Course info

For Platform 10 design is about making future change a part of the present. The design approach is characterised by a thoughtful exploration combining imagination with anticipation. With a strong social bias, curiosity for technology, and an appreciation of cultural insights the platform supports designers that are interested in extrapolating from their personal world into the universal. The key interest of the platform is in designs that challenge paradigms and offer new typologies.

(Source: www.rca.ac.uk)

The Vehicle Design Department encourages its students to understand the broader issues of vehicle design and to become aware of a range of issues that affect mobility, including: accessibility, aerodynamics, environmental impact, ergonomics, legislation, materials, production, safety and technology, and aesthetic principles. Since its foundation in 1967, the department has strongly influenced this field of product design. Early graduates went on to devise cars such as the Audi Quattro (Martin Smith), the Aston Martin DB7 (Ian Callum, Head of Design at Jaguar) and the Porsche 911 (Tony Hatter).

Candidates are selected on merit for acceptance by the Royal College of Art. They have to show proven design talent, together with the commitment and the ambition to succeed. Applicants will normally be aged over 21 years and have a high-level, relevant undergraduate degree and a substantial portfolio of work. Individual departments may have specific criteria that they expect you to meet, and you'll be competing against some of the finest graduates from both UK and overseas universities. On the plus side, a postgraduate qualification from the RCA is reliable currency within the design world – this is the home of the design superstars. Also, the college holds annual graduate summer shows where students display their work; these attract many of the movers and shakers in the design and manufacturing worlds who are keen to find new talent.

We've looked at a range of product design courses in some detail to highlight their diversity. If you are interested in this discipline, you'll need to plan your career path carefully and decide at an early stage whether you want broad-based study or more targeted training that will help you get into a particular type of work. You'll also need to research the available courses thoroughly to make sure you find one that is appropriate to your skills and interests.

⦿ Take action

- If you're planning to produce your own bespoke goods, or to go into small-scale manufacture, explore some of the websites we've referred to in this chapter, such as Etsy and Folksy.

- Keep designing and making – your portfolio needs to be up to date.

- Think carefully about the type of career structure you want. If you're thinking about industrial product design, you'll need to choose a relevant course that gives you a grounding in the field of expertise you want to focus on. Check out different courses by visiting university websites.

- If you're already at university/college, look at graduate recruitment programmes. Some of these have been hit badly by the recession, but there are still opportunities that could lead to a career in design. Start by looking at large organisations and multinationals that work in areas that interest you.

Chapter Four
EXHIBITION DESIGN

Exhibition design is three-dimensional: it involves working with a space to create a suitable platform for a display of some type and making that space attractive for people to visit. There is a more detailed definition of this discipline in Chapter 2.

To understand the range of careers available in exhibition design, you need to be aware of the many different types of exhibitions people visit. Here are a few examples – you'll probably be able to think of many more.

■ Museums and art galleries – part of the so-called 'heritage industry', these combine both permanent and temporary exhibitions; for example, every year major museums will stage a number of travelling shows in addition to their regular collections. Because many of these institutions are publicly funded they have to watch their costs. Employing in-house designers may not be cost-effective so they put their design and build contracts out to tender to companies that specialise in this area.

■ Leisure and visitor centres – whether you're going to the Sellafield Visitor Centre to see how nuclear processing works, or taking a trip to Alton Towers, you'll be going to an environment that has been designed to provide a fulfilling experience for visitors.

Here one of the country's most successful exhibition design companies describes its work.

We create physical and digital destinations where consumers can assimilate values and messaging, make purchases and enjoy time with brands. This is design with true intent – the creation of a space that expresses an attitude and personality while meeting clearly defined functional demands. It demands the development of a visual concept and, subsequently, its interpretation into three dimensions, down to the last detail. That fusion between concept and function is vital. From arrival through engagement to departure, the experience speaks to the subconscious as well as to the conscious mind. The impression made by colours and materials is just as important as ease of use in creating positive perceptions.
(Imagination, www.imagination.com)

■ Commercial in-house exhibitions – large organisations may stage permanent or semi-permanent displays at their premises to show clients what they do. These range from mini-museums in some of the major banks to interactive product demonstrations in the headquarters of manufacturing companies.

■ Trade exhibitions – every year, hundreds of exhibitions are staged across the world so that organisations can promote their goods and services. In this country alone, the National Exhibition Centre in Birmingham hosted 98 temporary trade exhibitions in 2008. These exhibitions are a marketplace and consequently exhibitors are working in direct physical competition with their rivals. You may be selling a product that can change the world but, in the crush and hubbub of a packed venue, nobody will be interested unless you can attract them to your exhibition stand. Hence the need for exhibition designers. Their task is to use a space (which is often very limited) to create an experience for visitors that highlights the client's offer.

We can't cover every area of exhibition design in this chapter so we're focusing on two specialist areas: temporary exhibition design and museum design.

TEMPORARY EXHIBITION DESIGN

The logistics of temporary exhibition design can be complex. Designers will not only be looking at aesthetic appeal, they also have to consider practicalities such as:

- cost – a client who is only exhibiting once a year probably won't want to spend a fortune on bespoke equipment like panels and lights

- portability – the stand and everything on it will have to be taken to the venue, erected and taken down in a short period of time

- accessibility – visitors have to be able to get on and off the stand easily, and exhibitors need the space to do their job. Designers have to be aware of potential footfall (the number of people who might walk on to the stand) and how many can be accommodated at one time

- health and safety – visitors to a stand aren't going to be impressed if they sprain an ankle tripping over fittings.

Design companies that specialise in this area may offer a range of services, from creating bespoke solutions to offering modular display solutions. They may have their own equipment (display board stands, projectors, lights, etc.) but most design companies hire these from specialist companies that will also take charge of building the stand.

It's worth noting, however, that many small to medium-sized organisations won't bother using a specialist temporary exhibition design agency if they only attend one or two trade fairs a year. Instead, they'll commission the design agency that they use for their marketing and promotional work

> As a three-dimensional marketing tool, exhibitions provide opportunities for brand development that are lacking in two-dimensional media. Held in a 'live' environment, temporary exhibitions are unusual in that they provide the designer with the scope to appeal to all the visitor's senses.
>
> (David Kelly, The Design Council)

to provide the service. Consequently, graphic designers may find that temporary exhibition design is another skill that they acquire.

Once the event is over, the designer may still have work to do. It can cost an organisation many thousands of pounds to stage a temporary exhibition, so there has to be a tangible result. Unless there is a quantifiable outcome in terms of the number of visitors to the stand, sales and positive new contacts, the financial investment will not be worthwhile. The client may ask the designer for some form of post-exhibition analysis that evaluates the success of the display and highlights areas for consideration for future exhibitions.

case STUDY

bluestone design is a multi-disciplined visual communications agency that offers creative branding and communication solutions to companies as diverse as supermarkets and high-tech engineering companies.

The company also regularly helps clients with display work. Managing Director Jonathan Armstead explains how bluestone diversified into this area.

'It was pure cheek on my part. We were doing brochure work for one of our major clients and I said I thought the graphics we'd done would look great as part of their display material. They had an exhibition coming up and we pitched for the work. We asked them what was their vision for the business – a question that nobody else had asked – and used that in our interpretation. We stood their display design concept on its head by creating a very open stand with its own environment that made them very approachable and matched the company's vision for the future. We had to find companies to work with, agree costs with the suppliers and the client, and then go out to both Germany and China. I oversaw the whole project in Germany and I had such a belief in what we were doing that I didn't let the client onto the stand until it was up and running. Later we took the exhibition to China, and had to negotiate with Chinese companies to do the installation. I was thinking on my feet all the time but I gained a lot of experience very quickly and it's an area of our business that's grown.'

Jonathan believes that this is an area of the design industry that will continue to grow, even in a financial downturn. 'It's a traditional method of selling. It may not be the most state-of-the-art, fashionable method, but people are leaning back on things that they know work. They're starting to re-evaluate marketing, and exhibitions are a key part of this. Companies are realising that they have to go out to get clients and give a window on what their businesses do.'

MUSEUM AND HERITAGE DESIGN

Jonothon Potter specialises in designing for museums, visitor centres, corporate public spaces and exhibitions. He is an illustrator by training and as part of his degree course at Middlesex University he worked on a placement at the National Maritime Museum in Greenwich. This started a lifelong passion for heritage work and a fascination for museums.

> *I was involved in designing an exhibition at the Public Records Office at Kew where we had to house documents such as the Domesday Book, the Magna Carta, Guy Fawkes' confession, the Dambusters' log book. It was the most incredible experience working with artefacts like these – you were handling things that related to some of the most important events in history.*

He's been involved with a number of projects, including exhibitions at St George's Hall, Liverpool, the National Coal Mining Museum for

England, and Power Station Earth in Iceland. He works closely with an exhibition design and build company that supplies technical equipment and expertise.

Jonothon believes that the focus of his business is 'telling a story':

> Don't look at a project from a mechanical aspect. You can't look at a piece of equipment and think 'I love this kit, I'm going to shoehorn it into the exhibition.' The story is king to everything and you have to design appropriately to that story. Some companies will follow the same design formula over and over again because they're comfortable with it, but it doesn't work.

Jonothon is passionate about his discipline. 'I love learning and I'm fascinated by museums. It's the simplicity of the objects that they house – someone created and made these things and there's a fascinating continuity of human endeavour when you work with them.'

Not that the work doesn't have its frustrations.

> There's a lot of preparation before you get a job – you have to understand the background to the exhibition and that might involve a lot of work. You may spend more of your time tendering for contracts and building relationships with potential clients than actually designing. And there's never enough time to do everything you want to. Plus, it's not a job where you can switch off – you're continually thinking about work. But the downsides are offset by my love for the work. If you enjoy learning and you want to be challenged by your work, then it's incredibly rewarding.

WHAT DOES IT TAKE TO SUCCEED?

There aren't many jobs in this area, but you can break into it if you take the initiative. Start building up a portfolio of your work as quickly as possible and include everything that might be relevant; remember that this type of design is interdisciplinary so you need to demonstrate an awareness of a range of techniques that contribute to effectively designing a space. Help out at your local museum, art gallery or stately home so that you get a clearer idea of the management issues that are involved. Learn as much as you can about what curators do and what standards they have to work to. All of this will contribute to your knowledge and can give you the edge if a job comes up.

An exhibition designer will need competences in a number of areas. Typically, an exhibition, whether temporary or permanent, will combine display components (pictures, graphics, etc.), furniture, open space and lighting to create an effect. They may also use sound, interactive games or struggling actors dressed in rabbit suits (seen at an exhibition for personnel development – don't ask why!). As a designer, you'll need to be able to work in three dimensions to manipulate space, so you may be using myriad design features, all of which you will need some knowledge about.

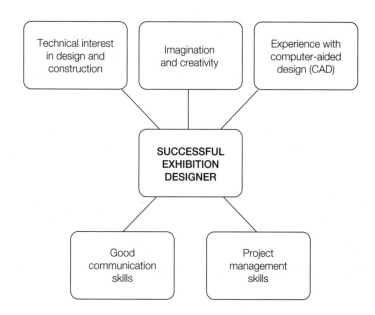

To succeed in this field, you need:

■ imagination and creativity – you're working in three dimensions and your clients will expect you to come up with innovative design solutions that use their expensive space effectively

■ an interest in the technical side of design and construction – you'll have to be aware of what materials work best in particular situations, how lighting can be used to create special effects, what electrical restrictions might limit your display...

■ good communication skills – as well as working with your client, you may have to supervise technical staff at the venue, negotiate with health and safety representatives, book equipment, etc.

■ experience with a range of computer-aided design (CAD) programs and a willingness to keep up with new developments

■ a firm grasp of project management techniques – your job is to produce a finished product (the exhibition) at a fixed time within a fixed budget. There is no scope for a job to over-run. You may have to bring together a number of different people (lighting engineers, display board providers, painters and decorators, promotions staff, etc.) at one time, so you should be organised yourself – and able to organise others.

Technology is changing all the time and we often bring in specialists to deal with specific areas of an exhibition such as lighting or interactive elements, but you still need to understand what's available.

(Jonothon Potter)

Flexibility is essential in this line of work, particularly if you're involved with temporary exhibitions. At large venues, they take place in rapid succession. If you're the designer, you may have a very limited time to erect and dismantle the stands – and you may have to work through the night. You may also be expected to stay around for the duration of the exhibition in case there are any problems or the client wants a change to the layout. Travel and antisocial hours are part of the job.

STARTING YOUR CAREER

Jonothon Potter moved into museum design from a career as an illustrator; bluestone has built up a lucrative business in delivering temporary exhibition solutions to a range of commercial clients, most of whom already used the company for marketing and branding design work.

Increasingly, however, people who want to work in this area will look for relevant educational opportunities rather than hoping to move into it via another design discipline. Institutions such as Lincoln School of Architecture offer specialist courses, such as the BA (Hons) Design for Exhibition and Museums. This course specialises in the design of 3D communicative environments that 'tell a story'.

Course info

On the [Exhibition and Design] programme students learn how to manipulate space and structure, design graphics (often to a large scale), storyboard multimedia and theatrical presentations, and have an understanding of the process of researching, writing and editing exhibition content to make it accessible to the required audience. This could be a technically sophisticated audience at a trade-only commercial exhibition or, by contrast, a mixed family group enjoying a day out at their local museum or visitor centre. In essence the programme produces designers who are 'storytellers' in three-dimensional space.

(Source: www.lincc.ac.uk)

As another example, the Salford Museum and Heritage Exhibition Design course also offers specialist training, and combines an understanding of current exhibition design practice with a range of business skills that practitioners will find essential.

If you don't want to follow a specialist course in exhibition design, other relevant courses include interior design and architecture, three-dimensional design and spatial design. Many students complete a one-year foundation course in art and design before moving into this area; this helps them to build a portfolio and to get a better idea of what the discipline involves.

The British Display Society (BDS) offers qualifications that you might want to explore, such as a two-year National Diploma in Retail Display Design and a one-year full-time General Certificate in Display. Its website (www.britishdisplaysociety.co.uk) gives details of the colleges where these courses are delivered.

Entry to degree courses is usually dependent on a minimum of two A-levels and five GCSEs (or equivalent) and a portfolio of work, though the academic qualifications may be waived for mature students and those with relevant experience or vocational qualifications.

Qualifications and/or experience in marketing and communications can also be useful – though obviously you'll need some proven talent for design as well!

There is no single, reliable source for job vacancies. You'll have to keep checking the Internet regularly (type 'jobs' + 'exhibition' + 'designer' into your search engine). You'll also find some openings advertised in trade magazines and professional journals that are relevant to your chosen field. Be prepared to enter the arena from an angle: you may find that a job with an advertising or communications agency gives you the start that you need.

Exhibition Designer

Salary £18K–23K. This is an established company with global offices/workshops that provides worldwide solutions for all their clients' exhibition requirements. The successful candidate will need to be experienced in relevant industry used software, i.e. 2D, 3D, AutoCAD and/or 3D VectorWorks, etc. Additional skills in Mac software such as Quark and Photoshop, etc., would be an advantage. You will be accountable for producing/working on designs for high-spec exhibition stands and modular displays.

Once you've started work in this field, what are the prospects like? There are a number of international companies, such as Imagination and Sarner, which have impressive track records in exhibition and display design, and employ a comparatively large number of design and technical staff. Another potential employment route is via in-house design teams in large organisations; retail chains, particularly those that focus on furniture or homeware and create distinct environments in their premises, may employ design staff who focus on exhibition and display work.

Many exhibition design specialists are located in London or near cities such as Manchester and Birmingham, where there are major exhibition venues.

Jonothon Potter thinks that the job ladder is more pertinent in this design discipline than in many others:

> When graduates come out of college they still have a lot to learn because there are so many aspects to this type of work. They have to work their way up. As junior designers, they will have a lot of catching up to do before they can progress to senior designer and then design manager, etc. I think it's fair to say that there's a fair rate of drop-out because many new designers find it hard to take the strain.

There are also many smaller specialist exhibition design companies, some of which will employ freelance designers for specific contracts. To become a freelance, you're going to need a proven track record and considerable experience within the industry. Many jobs are passed on by word of mouth, so reputation is very important.

Once you're established, you'll still need to keep up with changes both in design techniques and exhibition trends. The Chartered Society of Designers, the professional organisation for designers from all disciplines, is a useful source of information on continuing professional development and publishes a members' magazine, *The Designer*.

◓ Take action

- Carry out a skills audit to find out what areas of competence you'll need to improve on if you're going to work in this field. Are your technical skills up to the job? Can you think in three dimensions?

- Visit as many permanent exhibitions as you can to see how they work. This is a discipline that is always changing, and the way that exhibition space is used in galleries and museums can be as exciting as the exhibits. Look at the way in which they are made interactive – this is a key feature in exhibitions that seek to educate and entertain.

- Go to some trade exhibitions and consider how designers use limited space to convey messages about their clients.

- Check out the range of courses available at colleges and universities to find out what they involve.

Chapter Five
FASHION AND TEXTILE DESIGN

Fashion and textile designers influence the way that we look – even if we consider ourselves impervious to fashion. The styles of clothes that we wear, the colours and fabrics we favour, the heel heights and handbag sizes that we find on the high street are the result of the fashion and textile designer's work. There's a detailed explanation of this discipline in Chapter 2.

FASHION DESIGN

From the day they started dressing up in their mother's (or father's) clothes, or choosing a special outfit for their dolls, some people have a special interest in fashion. Whereas for most of us clothes are something that we use to enhance our appearance, to the dedicated few they are an obsession. Visualising them, designing them, making them – it's something that these people desperately want to do.

These are the fashion designers who, despite knowing that successful careers in this field are rarer than hens' teeth, are determined to carve out a role for themselves.

Fashion designers work in a number of fields. They may design clothes, shoes or accessories (or all three). At the top end of the scale, those who work with the major couture houses design one-off pieces that can sell for thousands of pounds. Working on a one-to-one basis with their affluent clients, they will organise fittings and supervise the creation of something special. At the same time, they will design ready-to-wear collections; the garments in these will be produced in small numbers so they retain their exclusivity.

At the other end of the scale, designers may work in a team creating mass-produced fashions for high-street stores and supermarkets, or specialist clothing for outdoors or sport. Garments are produced in large numbers, often in factories overseas where labour is cheaper. The imperative for these designers isn't so much about producing something distinctive and special but about meeting strict budgeting and manufacturing targets. Forget the hand-finishing and fancy, twiddly bits; these clothes must be produced in their thousands for minimal cost so that they can be in the stores by a particular date.

In an interview in the *Guardian* in January 2009, fashion designer Sarah Davis described her work. She is responsible for designing the entire girlswear range for Asda's George label. With three assistants, she is expected to design about 300 different items of clothing for each six-month season. Her work involves a fair amount of travel as she searches for inspiration and visits suppliers, but otherwise she is based on an industrial estate in Leicestershire and works fairly normal office hours.

If you have aspirations to be a designer, you may be able to carve out a career that is challenging and incredibly exciting. But remember that there is only one Alexander McQueen and one Stella McCartney. Your chances of developing your own fashion label are very, very slight. Having said that, it can be done, if you have the determination – and the talent – to succeed.

Fashion guru Matthew Williamson was offered a place on the fashion design degree course at Central Saint Martins, London, when he was only 17.

case STUDY

He graduated in 1994, then freelanced for Marni before going to work for Monsoon and Accessorize. He and his business partner, Joseph Velosa, launched Matthew Williamson Ltd in 1997 with a debut show that featured models of the calibre of Jade Jagger, Kate Moss and Helena Christensen. He was *Elle* Designer of the Year in 2004, and received the 2005 Moët and Chandon Fashion Tribute, as well as being nominated three times for the Designer of the Year at the British Fashion Awards.

So mega-stardom does happen in the fashion industry. But for the rest of the profession, the rise to fame and fortune may be a little more measured.

The responsibilities of a designer vary according to the size and type of company they work for. They may be expected to do any or all of the following.

- Produce ideas and concepts for individual items and full ranges of products.

- Draw their concepts by hand or on the computer so that others can interpret them.

- Develop patterns.

- Manage the production process, including overseeing manufacture and quality control.

- Help with the merchandising of products by contributing to fashion shows and helping stores display them.

Fashion is one of the fastest-moving industries in the world. Forty years ago, most men and women would expect to buy one or two new items for winter and summer. Clothes, particularly coats, suits, shoes and handbags, were expensive and considered to be a major financial investment. Now, in relative terms, clothes have become much cheaper, and we can replenish our wardrobes for every season. Check out any of the popular fashion magazines and you'll see that many fashion businesses are promoting ranges of clothes for winter, spring, summer and autumn.

TEXTILE DESIGN

Last season it was tartan, this season geometrics, next it could be florals. This year blue is the new black; next year black may be the new black. Textiles, which are an intrinsic part of our lives and play a key role in the fashion statements that we make, change all the time.

Textile designers not only create designs for knitted, printed and woven fabrics that go into clothes manufacture, but they also design textiles for household fabrics and furnishings, and for technical products such as specialist outdoor clothing. They need to have detailed knowledge of how fabrics are produced, their properties and how they can be used before they start considering the aesthetic elements of design. Because of this, they will work closely with clients in whatever area they specialise in before they produce design ideas.

There are a number of illuminating case studies written by textile designers on Prospects, the UK's official graduate careers website (www.prospects.ac.uk). These are worth looking at, because they highlight the range of careers that these designers have built and also some of the problems – in particular the isolation and the difficulties of running a business as well as designing – which are faced by those who are self-employed.

WHAT DOES IT TAKE TO SUCCEED?

Of all the design disciplines, this is one of the hardest to break into. Not only will you be up against thousands of other talented, aspiring designers, you'll also be competing for a very limited number of opportunities.

The diagram below shows the qualities needed to be a successful fashion designer.

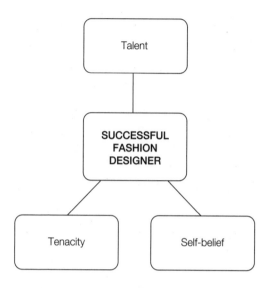

London is the centre of the fashion industry, though there are successful businesses in other large cities, such as Manchester. Most design companies, including the very successful ones, are small enterprises; they will employ two or three designers and contract out all their manufacturing work.

Because competition for places in these companies is so fierce, anyone wanting to break into the world of fashion design needs to consider approaching it from another angle.

You also need a lot of energy. Fashion designers work long hours, especially when collections are being prepared. Yes, you may get to travel to fashion shows around the world – but that in itself can be hard work. This isn't a job that lends itself to a stable home life and getting home to meet the kids when they finish school.

Lucy Gledhill got a job in retail when she graduated from her fashion degree course

'When you're at university, you're encouraged to be this brilliant, innovative, reinventing-the-wheel designer. There was never a point when I felt grounded, where somebody pointed out that there weren't that many jobs out there. So after I graduated I got a job in retail doing visual merchandising. I still rely on that experience in my career now. You can design a collection of clothes, but you've also got to think about what they'll look like on the rail in the shop – will a customer want to buy them?'

(Lucy Gledhill, fashion designer, Hooch)

Just back from a fashion show in Barcelona, Lucy says, 'It sounds glamorous, and yes, I get to do a lot of shopping. But I walk for miles, spend a lot of time in cramped airplane seats, work until 9 pm most nights, and at weekends. And the money isn't great. But I really love what I do – and that makes it worthwhile.'

As well as creative talent, it will help if you have gained some technical skills such as pattern cutting and garment construction. Although you may never be asked to make a garment yourself, your designs will need to be informed by technical knowledge because this influences the cost of the finished product. If a dress design is too complicated, uses too much fabric or takes too long to finish, then it will not be profitable – and, as with all industries, the fashion business exists to make a profit.

You'll also have to be aware of changing trends in fashion, fabrics and lifestyle. Collections are usually prepared two seasons in advance, so as autumn 2009 begins you'll be thinking about clothes for summer 2010. Predicting the future is a tricky business, so designers who don't have a crystal ball will spend a lot of time researching factors that might have an influence on fashion trends. They will often liaise with buyers and marketing executives before starting to produce designs so that their ideas are in line with the retail plans of major clients.

Lucy now works for Hooch, an innovative brand that is popular worldwide. Working in a team of two, she designs 300–400 pieces a year. One of her responsibilities is recruiting students for work experience. So what does she look for?

> We want people who are eager to listen and understand the commercial aspect of the work. A lot of people who come in think they know it all – as I think I did as a student – and they don't realise how much of a business it is. They've got to learn to make money for someone else and to make someone else want to buy their products. They have to learn to manipulate their customers. Ideally I want to see someone who has a freshness and new ideas about how to do that.

Lucy herself, despite being only 25 years old, is also considering her own future:

> You're only good for a few years in this business unless you go into management or consultancy. I've probably only got another 10 years in this type of job. I haven't any ambition to get my own line going, because my strength is reinterpreting high fashion looks to a broader fashion market. And I don't think everyone has to be Alexander McQueen. I'd be interested in going into teaching on a course like the one I was on at Manchester.

Textile designers need many of the same qualities of tenacity and talent. As well as having an eye for colour, texture and pattern, they'll also need extensive technical knowledge about fabric production methods. Textiles will be produced in bulk for the mass market; at the luxury end of the market, however, there is a demand for specialist textiles ranging from hand embroidery to silk-screen prints. However, this demand is very limited and unlikely to earn you a living unless you become very successful.

Because this type of work is so closely related to the needs of clients, communication skills are particularly important. As a textile designer, you will be interpreting customers' requirements, and they may not know exactly what they want a fabric to do. Consequently, you'll be involved in detailed discussions about the performance of the textile, as well as cost and production methods. Producing a textile that doesn't exactly meet the requirements can be disastrous if the problems are not addressed before products are made up.

As with all design disciplines, an awareness of business and management principles is essential. You will need to understand budgets and project management techniques, to make presentations and negotiate contracts, particularly if you work freelance or for a small design company.

STARTING YOUR CAREER

Back in the 1960s, fashion design icon Paul Smith started his career in a Nottingham clothing warehouse. In 1970, he opened a boutique in the same town, took evening classes in tailoring and within six years was showing his first menswear collection in Paris.

You'll still find examples of people who've burst on the scene by similarly unusual methods, but increasingly in the qualifications-obsessed twenty-first century, fashion designers follow a more conventional route through education.

After completing a GNVQ in Art and Design as well as A-levels, Lucy studied for a BA in Fashion at Manchester Metropolitan University. There are a lot of courses available and it's important to choose one that offers you the technical skills and creative outlets you want. Ideally, a course will also give you some grounding in business principles so that you can approach the industry with a level head.

For degree and HNC/HND courses, you'll need to fulfil minimum educational requirements (usually three A-levels or equivalent) and present a portfolio to show that you have the talent to merit a place. Many establishments will insist that you complete a foundation course in art and design before specialising in fashion; look at individual university and college websites to find out their precise requirements. Remember that because competition for jobs is high, employers will expect their staff to have gained the technical skills they need at college, so make sure that somewhere in your education you cover these.

Graduates from many different colleges get their first chance to show their work at Graduate Fashion Week in London. As well as stands, they may get a chance to publicise their portfolios and contribute to a catwalk show – and this is an occasion that attracts a lot of industry talent-spotters.

The MA Fashion course at Central Saint Martins College of Art and Design, under the direction of the iconic Professor Louise Wilson, is probably the most respected fashion course in the world. If you can get a place on this – and have the talent and stamina to get through its rigorous demands – you stand a chance of joining the brightest and best in British fashion. Students follow one of its pathways in womenswear, menswear, knitwear, textiles, fashion journalism or accessories.

Alumni include:

- 1993, Alister Mackie, Fashion Director of Another Man and menswear consultant for Lanvin and Fendi

- 1997, Natasa Cagalj, Head of Design at Stella McCartney

- 1998, Marc Weston, Menswear Design Director at Burberry

- 2000, Todd Lynn, worked for Roland Mouret before starting his own label

- 2001, Jonathan Kirby, Senior Design Director at Levi

- 2006, Christopher Kane, renowned own label and consultant for Lanvin

And that's just a sample. It's an amazing place, and everyone, but everyone, in the fashion business respects its achievements. However, it only accepts 25 students a year on the MA Fashion course. If you're brave enough to think of applying, check out the website at www.csm.arts.ac.uk.

Once you've qualified and got that all-important first job, you'll spend a lot of time learning from more experienced designers. You may spend your first few years in a very junior position, working on other people's designs.

But if you continue to develop your own portfolio at the same time, this experience will stand you in good stead.

Fashion design is a hard field to break into and many would-be graduates have found their first position through word of mouth or contacts that they've made when they were studying. However, there are some published vacancies out there on websites such as www.fashionunited. co.uk and (occasionally) in publications such as the *Guardian*.

Design Co-ordinator/Assistant Designer

Salary: £24K–32K. London. We are looking for a Design Co-ordinator/Assistant Designer for a women's lifestyle fusion label. With a strong design background, you will possess a flair and appreciation for creative design. We are particularly interested in applicants who have experience designing for the independent market (specialising in the 35+ age group) for women who are looking for something 'a little different' to the high-street offering. Reporting to the Design Director, you will need to demonstrate excellent visualisation skills, help to oversee and co-ordinate the entire product ranges from start to finish, range planning, visiting factories overseas if necessary. You will integrate original ideas from our design team into spec sheets accurately and be able to hand-illustrate as well as using Photoshop and Illustrator.

Assistant Children's Wear Designer

An exciting opportunity has arisen for a talented and trend-led Children's Wear Designer to join one of the UK's best-known retailers. You will need at least two years' postgraduate commercial design experience working on baby wear and girls wear. You will be able to interpret women's and men's trends to children's wear, have a good understanding of garment construction and high-street supply. Strong CAD skills are highly desirable.

Here are a couple of examples. They give you a flavour of the type of experience employers are looking for – and the packages they are offering.

Many educational establishments, such as University College Falmouth and London Metropolitan University, now offer specialist undergraduate and postgraduate courses in textile design. As with all higher education courses, you'll be expected to have qualifications at A-level (or equivalent). The courses vary in content, but most will train you in a range of skills that enable you to understand the principles of fabricating textiles from conception through to final production. A comprehensive source of advice on these courses is www.hotcourse.com.

If you're still at school, it's worth exploring new vocational qualifications such as GNVQ and Special Diplomas that encourage a combination of practical creative application and theory. The diplomas are particularly useful in that they include elements on business and highlight the processes that practitioners will be involved in when they start work.

Textile designers work in many different types of companies, ranging from design studios to textile mills. Again, there is a lot of competition for vacancies and it's important to widen your job search as far as possible. You may want to design textiles for high fashion – but you may find that there are more openings for designers who produce textiles for soft furnishings or workwear.

Because the range of companies that employ textile designers is fairly broad and includes textile manufacturers, vacancies exist in areas other than London and the south east. Although the textile industry has declined in the north of England, a number of large companies have maintained their bases in Yorkshire, Lancashire, other parts of the North-west, Scotland and the East Midlands. There may also be opportunities to work overseas with companies that are based in the Far East or in Europe.

As with fashion design, one way of getting started is to take on any work experience that you can find, even if this is unpaid. Retail experience can broaden your understanding of the demands on the designer and keep you abreast of new trends. At the same time, you must keep working on your portfolio – it is this that will help you to stand out from other candidates when you apply for a job.

◉ Take action

■ Check out trade and general fashion magazines. Whether you're aiming to work in high fashion or high-street fashion, you need to keep abreast of the trends. You should be reading the major fashion magazines – *Vogue*, *Elle*, etc. – on a regular basis. It's interesting to compare these against some of the mass-market weeklies like *Look* and *More* to see how trends are translated into the high street.

■ Visit trade fairs. You may not be able to get a personal invitation to London Fashion Week, but you can visit many of the industry fairs that take place around the country. You can find listings on the websites of individual venues like the National Exhibition Centre, Birmingham, and Olympia in London. www.drapersonline.com has a monthly calendar of shows worldwide.

■ Keep adding to your portfolio. Styles change so quickly in fashion that your portfolio will need to be up to date. A prospective employer won't be interested in designs you sketched two years ago.

■ Improve your practical skills – pattern-cutting, dressmaking, textile production. The more competent you are, the more valuable you are to an organisation.

Chapter Six
GRAPHIC DESIGN

Graphic designers communicate messages visually using typography, lettering and illustration. They design a wide range of products, from brochures and books through to packaging and labels. There's a more detailed description of this discipline in Chapter 2.

A PROUD TRADITION

It is arguable that graphic design began when the first artists started drawing pictures of stick men and animals in caves in places like Lascaux. Certainly, the development of written language in the third or fourth millennium BCE was a significant milestone in the history of graphic design. For hundreds of years, books were handwritten and illustrated and provided examples of exquisite artistry – but they were seen by only a few people. The introduction of movable type and the mass production of printed material in the seventeenth century was a major step forward, but it wasn't until the nineteenth century that graphic design and related applied arts gained real popularity.

William Morris helped to pioneer the separation of design from production and from fine art. From 1891 to 1896 his Kelmscott Press published graphic design products for the Arts and Crafts movement. He made beautiful books that he could sell for a very high price – as well as designing wallpaper in styles that remain fashionable today.

In the early twentieth century, a number of designers began to explore new styles of font and layout, and graphic design gained the hold over our senses that it retains today. Even now, we are familiar with the railway posters of the 1930s, and the early covers of Ordnance Survey maps. These designs combined a number of graphic features that created unforgettable images.

Twentieth-century advances in computers, photography and printing techniques have revolutionised graphic design, particularly in the way that it now allows for mass production. We live in a world where rapid, high-impact communications have gained precedence over more measured forms. Back in the 1960s, a famous Canadian communications guru, Marshall McLuhan, first stated that 'the medium is the message'. He was referring to advertising, which he described as 'the greatest art form of the twentieth century', but his idea is relevant to every form of visual communication. We're as interested in the method of communication as the communication itself.

Advertising and other forms of communications media have changed the way we live through combining images and words in ways that seduce us or manipulate our opinions. None of this could happen without a pool of talented graphic designers who can contribute the visuals.

Graphic designers specialise in visual communications – they communicate a message to an audience using some form of visual representation such as pictures, drawings, photographs, logos, colour, etc. Because this form of communication supports almost all the messages that we receive, graphic designers are employed in many different areas and their work often overlaps into some of the other design disciplines that we're looking at in this book. So, for example, a website designer will

> Graphic design is everywhere from bands to brands, CDs to seed packets, fashion magazines to free sheets, T-shirts to tea bags, pop promos to pop-up books and websites to building sites. Graphic designers create work which informs, persuades, entertains and sells through the organisation of image, type, materials and processes. Every day you are bombarded by thousands of graphic design images, messages and ideas, from the moment you open your cornflakes until the last TV ad or website you see before you close your eyes to sleep.
>
> (Source: www.mdx.ac.uk)

use (or buy in) graphic design skills. A fashion designer who is putting together a new portfolio may ask a graphic designer to help him or her create a strong visual image. An agency that specialises in brand design will use graphic designers to create publicity materials, new logos, etc. An exhibition designer will use graphic design skills to prepare a display that combines words, colours and images to their best effect so that it attracts an audience.

WHAT DOES IT TAKE TO SUCCEED?

In the old days (that's not actually very long ago) many graphic designers sketched out their ideas using archaic instruments called pencils and markers. They created storyboards to show what the finished product would look like, and they relied on specialists like typesetters and printers to do the technical work. Now the process is almost completely computerised. Yes, some graphic designers prefer to start a job with hand-drawn visuals, but most will work on a computer, using specialised industry-standard graphics and multimedia software packages. These programs can produce artwork that, when it is approved, can go straight to the printers.

Modern graphic design has evolved into a profession that is undertaken almost entirely on computers. It is not a career for technophobes. It demands highly developed technical skills – most designers will have experience using a number of different programs such as Quark, Illustrator, InDesign and Freehand. Employers will expect potential new recruits to have the relevant skills, as this advertisement shows.

Graphic Designer

Salary £24K–30K. This design company with own print/ production facility is now seeking an additional versatile graphic designer to join its existing team. You will be fully Mac-literate, have experience of working with Quark, Illustrator, InDesign and Freehand, and have a proven track record in working on a broad mix of accounts and briefs. Duties will include taking projects from concept through to completion.

There is a problem with this reliance on technology, however. Because anyone can access design software and use templates to produce visuals, there's a tendency to think that anyone can be a graphic designer. Not true. To be a successful graphic designer, you need a lot of talent, a strong creative 'eye', an ability to draw and an understanding of how space, colour and typography can be manipulated to create an effect. No computer package is going to replace innate ability.

Graphic designers will usually work with a number of other people, such as copywriters, photographers and account managers. Generally, the process for getting a job off the ground will be something like this.

- The account manager (if the agency has one) and the designer talk to the client to find out what they want (not always an easy task, as they often don't know).

- From this meeting, they will prepare a 'brief' that lays out what is required. It's useful to have firm guidelines written down at an early stage so that the client doesn't keep changing his or her mind.

- The designer may work with the account manager to prepare budgets and time frames, as well as drafting the visual input.

- The designer will put together draft design ideas for the client to comment on. This may involve considerable research, a process that the Internet has made much easier. Designers no longer have to leave their studios and spend hours trawling libraries to get inspiration.

- Once a concept has been agreed, there will usually be a presentation to the client to give some idea of the finished product. Clients often ask more than one design agency to pitch for work so that they can get the best deal.

- The final design will be created and amended if necessary. Usually this stage of the work will be done to strict deadlines – once clients have made a decision about what they want, they are likely to demand delivery 'yesterday'.

- Once the design is 'signed off' by the client and cannot be changed, the designer may supervise sending it to print.

Of course, there are dozens of variations on this scenario. Some agencies will have production managers who liaise with printers and other technical experts. Some companies only allow account managers to deal directly with clients. Freelance designers will do everything themselves – from initial talks with the client through to driving round the finished product.

What all this suggests is that graphic designers have to be flexible and prepared to take on whatever tasks are required of them.

Obviously, underlying these skills, you need to have a degree of creative talent, a strong visual sense and a passion for presentation. Because graphic design impacts so heavily on all our lives, the quest for originality and for something really eye-catching is particularly competitive – but if you have the power to think 'outside the box' *and* meet your client's needs, you should have a successful career.

Ian Loseby of Arris describes the process that he works through when he's working on a design project.

> *Ideas might come in a split second – I've done logos quite quickly and at other times I've spent days and not succeeded. I research hard and see what other people, including the client's competition, have done. I look through general design references and pick out the elements that help my vision. Do I want big letters on this? Do I want photographs? Do I want knock-back or a foreground thing? Sometimes I'll see something small that will make a massive impact.*
>
> *From my research I end up with 20 or 30 written ideas and lots of little drawings or doodles. I'm constantly going back to basics and thinking about the people, the company and the market. Once I've got the overall feel that I want, there may be two or three fundamental ideas that I can start breaking down. We show the client a maximum of three ideas; any more and we'll faze them.*
>
> *The biggest problem is getting the client to make a decision, so I start by asking which of the three ideas they like the least, and then we're down to two. Invariably people want to mix and match – they want a bit of that concept and bit of that one. Often they're scared*

of making a decision. Once you've agreed the basic concept you can start looking at typefaces, colours, etc.; then you can make a presentation.

As with all the other design fields that we're investigating, business skills are important. Your client will only have a certain budget to play with and will want work to be completed to meet deadlines (which often seem very short). As a graphic designer, you'll be expected to appreciate the importance of these constraints. You'll also need powerful communication skills, not only to communicate ideas to clients but also to help you prepare design briefs and work with other team members.

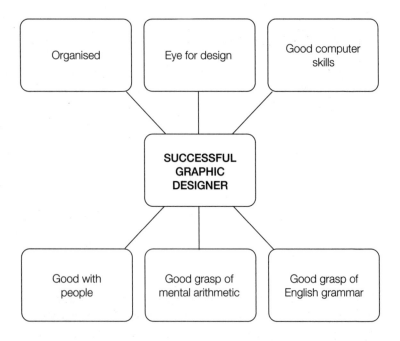

Graphic designer Conrad Stead says:

If I were recruiting a new designer, I'd look for:

■ *a good eye for design – someone who's interested and can differentiate between what's good and what's not*

■ *good Mac/computer skills*

- *someone who's organised about their work and keeps up with the paperwork*
- *a good grasp of English, grammar and punctuation*
- *mental arithmetic – you need this to work out spacings and placings when you're typesetting or laying out a page*
- *someone who is personable and good with people; you don't need to be particularly outgoing, but you do need to be approachable, a good listener and patient*
- *someone with interests outside college or work that shows me they have persistence and focus to see a project through.*

GETTING STARTED

Graphic designer Chris Craddock has the following advice for anyone thinking of a career in graphic design:

> *IT skills and computers have made everyone think that they are designers. Being able to fit everything in and make a page look tidy is NOT design – you have to have the right talent, skills and training. I'd suggest that anyone considering this field should take an introductory graphic design course that includes print procedure (so that you know what you're designing for), typography, life drawing and packaging. Then decide on your career path and complete a minimum two further years in your specific area.*

There are plenty of courses on offer, ranging from of NVQs/SVQs in design subjects and Foundation Diplomas in Art and Design, through to undergraduate and postgraduate courses in graphic design, illustration, fine art or a related subject. Because the choice is so great, you really need to do your homework before choosing a course. Read prospectuses carefully and look for testimonials from students to get a flavour of the course content. The BA Honours Graphic Design at Middlesex University, an establishment that is renowned for its design work, offers students modules on graphic design, advertising, magazine design, photography, typography, TV graphics and web design.

If I were looking for a new recruit to a graphic design team, above all I'd want enthusiasm, flexibility and a feeling for design. Technically, I'd expect them to be able to produce designs to customer specifications, be able to draw, select typefaces and come up with colour combinations. In terms of IT, they should be familiar with Mac and design software, like Q16. Ideally I'd look for someone who's been out of college for at least a year and has some studio work or freelance experience.

(Chris Craddock, Creative Link)

Ironically, the increase in the number of graphic design courses and opportunities to study related subjects means that, despite the growth in demand for designers, competition for jobs is as stiff as ever. There are a lot of young graduates out there desperate to make their mark. It's essential that, as well as an education, you get as much work experience as you can, and continually build your portfolio.

Advertising, media, PR and communications agencies all employ graphic designers. The terminology for the 'picture people' in these organisations can be confusing. We'll make some generalisations here, but don't be surprised if you find different titles for similar jobs when you get out into the market.

A creative director, or senior creative, will develop the visual element of a campaign. They will usually work directly with the client to translate their needs into a viable format. Because these people need to think visually, and to understand the production processes, many senior creative staff have worked their way up from more lowly positions as graphic designers or illustrators.

The creative director will brief the others who contribute to the product, such as the copywriter and the visualisers. Their job is to translate the initial idea onto paper, and to produce rough designs and layouts that will be developed into finished artwork using a combination of drawing, typography and photography. An agency may also use illustrators who specialise in hand-drawn illustrations – although these are an increasingly rare breed.

Computer technology has revolutionised design, and today visualisers will do most of their work on computer. Producing the finished artwork is a skilled and specialist job – you will often see vacancies advertised for 'Mac operators', whose responsibility will be to take mock-ups and draft drawings and produce print-ready designs.

It's not easy to get your first break, but a lot of agencies use graphic designers and may be willing to offer you at least a temporary post. Also, some large organisations, such as publishers, retailers, local and central government departments, still have in-house design teams so you should spread your job-hunting net as wide as possible. Surf the Internet – there are a number of online recruitment agencies that specialise in graphic design vacancies.

Junior Designer

Salary £13K–14K. Graphic design company seeks an enthusiastic and talented designer to join its studio. This role is ideal for someone wanting to develop their graphic design skills, and who is enthusiastic and willing to deal with customers face to face and over the telephone. You will be responsible for advising customers on products; you will take part in monthly networking meetings and be required to help with invoicing, quoting, etc. Your primary objective is the graphic design skill.

Many graphic designers eventually work for themselves, either as freelancers or in small partnerships. The nature of the work means that it lends itself to self-employment: graphic designers have low overheads (you can work from home as long as you have a good computer and Internet access) and it's a field where commissions are often the result of personal recommendations.

Self-employment can be a tempting option, particularly if you work as a senior creative with an agency and want more freedom – and a bigger share of the money that is being paid for a design job. It is also an option that many people at all levels are considering now, at a time when unemployment is rising and the number of available jobs is shrinking.

Chris Craddock now runs his own business, Creative Link, but during his long and varied career he has worked in a number of capacities for design and communications agencies. Here he describes some aspects of his working life.

case
STUDY

'An art teacher at school sparked my interest in graphic design. After studying the subject at college, I went to work for the Department of Employment (as it was then) as a display and exhibition designer to get people into work. I was a one-man band, designing, generating and producing everything myself using outsourced reproduction houses and printers, etc.

'Next I worked as a finishing artist in an advertising design studio, producing artwork from the visualisers' designs. I moved up to become studio manager, managing a studio of about 20 people, and then an account manager where I designed, visualised, liaised with clients and managed budgets. Over the next few years I was a design consultant/account director for a number of advertising agencies, then became creative director of an in-house design studio for a management training company. Finally I decided to go freelance and now work as a visualiser, designer, illustrator and cartoonist under the trading name Creative Link.

'I work mostly from home although occasionally, when I'm working for an advertising agency, I work in-house at their premises. If I'm at home in my studio, I typically work in two- to three-hour bursts through the day, with breaks in between. If necessary I work in the evening, and if I'm involved with a big job, I work late at night for as long as it takes to meet a deadline.

'Although I work for myself, I'm usually part of a team working on a project. I design and generate Mac-based page layouts, then there'll be a copywriter and a Mac operator with a bigger and better system than mine, who can generate larger outputs and follow design visuals. We also work with a print company. The project team is permanent (all freelancers who've worked together for years), although printers vary according to what the finished product is. For example, we may use a specialist company for exhibition panels, embossing and special effects such as cut-outs.

'The work is very varied – and that's where a lot of the pleasure lies. You can get really involved in what you're doing and you get a lot of satisfaction from the finished product. For example, recently a client, who creates automated Christmas displays and Santa's grottos in shopping malls round the country, phoned and requested a meeting. I went to their premises to take a brief that laid out what they wanted, the format they wanted it in, timescales for the job, cost estimates, etc. The theme was a Victorian Christmas street scene. They wanted large visuals of the scene with Victorian Christmas decorations, incorporating automated teddy bears doing various activities that could be fabricated and mechanised easily. It wasn't just a question of coming up with interesting creative ideas; I had to understand the mechanical constraints of the activities, so that the client could easily mechanise the automatons to perform the action. The client provided some references – visuals of similar work on paper, CD and video – and we verbally agreed a cost estimate. My next step was researching and collecting other references from books, Google Images and from my own photographs of Victorian shopfronts, windows and railings. I used these as the basis for my drawings.

'I produced rough visuals in pencil, scanned them and emailed them to the client for comment and approval. Sometimes I have to redraw elements in line with the client's comments, but in this case the rough drawings were approved straight away. I then had to produce five A2 storyboards and get them approved. Finally, I could send in my invoice!

'That's the creative part of my work. The business and administration side are also very important. I'm running a business, and I have to keep hold of everything from invoicing and financial control through to marketing. About 10% of my time is spent on administration – although that goes up to 99% for the week before my tax return is due! I think that anyone who wants to work for themselves has to understand the importance of business, admin and management skills. Time management is essential because you have to deliver work promptly, and communication skills are key so that you work effectively both with your clients and the rest of the project team.

'There are times when business can seem very uncertain, so you have to be flexible. Then, without warning, you'll get a commission that you really enjoy. When I started out, I really just wanted to design album covers – and finally, after years in the business working on commercial contracts, I've just been asked to do one!

'I'd advise anyone who wants to succeed as a graphic designer to keep up to date, knowledgeable and interested in the field because design is constantly changing. Read and collect art, design and typography magazines and books, both retro and new, to generate ideas. Practise and experiment on your own projects. The Internet has revolutionised research. Google is fantastic as a reference and image resource so you can work from home rather than trekking to libraries and searching out photo references, so there's no excuse for not staying in touch with new trends.'

⊘ Take action

- How much do you really know about graphic design? Start your own research project into different areas of the discipline, such as the development of typography.

- Build up your competence in using relevant software – you'll need to be proficient. Explore new packages that are coming on the market – traditional ones such as PageMaker are rapidly being replaced.

- Check out university and college courses to see how their content varies. If you're not at a point where you can go into full-time education, look for evening classes in graphic design or related fields.

- Start building up a portfolio and keep it up to date – this will be your main selling point when you start looking for a job.

Chapter Seven
INTERACTIVE
MEDIA DESIGN

If you tell someone that you're an interior designer, they'll probably have a fairly good idea of the work that you do. But if you say that you're an interactive media designer, be prepared for blank stares unless you're talking to someone who works in the same field.

If you work in interactive media you may design websites, computer games, online advertisements, music videos, educational software… This is a term that is famously difficult to define because it applies to an industry that is constantly changing. As each piece of technology is replaced by something newer and more versatile, so the demand on designers' skills changes.

The boundaries between interactive media and other forms of digital media are not clear-cut. Because computer technology dominates our lives, interactive media supports many areas of our lives, from education through to e-commerce.

You'll find designers working in almost every industry and service sector, providing everything from eye-catching e-marketing devices for retail organisations, to billing management options for utility companies, to customer service interfaces for banks. Consequently, discussing careers in this discipline is tricky: we can't possibly cover all the different areas, and we're going to make some generalisations. It will be up to you to research the particular field that interests you.

In broad terms, the work of an interactive media designer is to produce visuals of the screens that users will access. The visuals will describe the look and feel of each element of the website/game/CD-ROM/user interface, so they'll include graphics, colour schemes, etc., and they may also show how the different elements respond when they are used. Think about your mobile phone: a designer somewhere will have come up with the layout for the homepage, then worked through the various sections in the menu to show what each screen will look like when you access the homepage options.

Few interactive media designers work solely on the visuals; many of them are also developers who will carry out the programming for their designs. Even if they work with dedicated programmers and information architects, they'll still need to understand how the product will be programmed so they can design to its capabilities.

WEBSITE DESIGNERS

One particular area of interactive media that has increased massively in popularity over the last few years is the website. Think about the last time you needed a particular product, service or piece of information. How did you find it? The chances are that you went straight to your laptop, went into Google or Yahoo, and looked for a relevant website.

In the last 20 years we've seen a radical change in the way that business operates. There are very few businesses today that don't have a website to publicise their work, act as a point of customer contact, and provide a commercial channel. Thousands of organisations now trade solely via the Internet, using their websites in place of conventional business premises. You might have your own website – or at least a 'mini website' on Facebook or Bebo. All of these websites – and there are millions of them – have to be designed and developed.

When the Internet was first invented, web design consisted of a very basic markup language that included some formatting options, and the unique ability to link pages together using hyperlinks. Now it is far more sophisticated – but an effective website observes the seven 'Cs' of web design.

■ Context: it has a distinctive look and feel, whether it is traditional, trendy, utilitarian or touchy-feely. This is created by its use of colour, graphics, visuals, images, etc.

■ Content: consistency in the digital material that it contains, including text, video, audio and graphics.

■ Community: it creates a feeling of membership and a strong sense of involvement among users so that they feel part of something.

■ Customisation: the site can tailor itself to a user or be personalised by users so it suits their needs.

■ Communication: there is clear communication between the site and the user.

■ Connection: the network of the site that links it to other sites.

■ Commerce: the activity that the site permits – the sale of goods and services.

A (VERY) LITTLE TECHNICAL INFORMATION

The technicalities of website design are complex if you're not already involved in this field, so we'll use an example of the types of site developed by a particular company to illustrate how the systems can work.

Labrys Multimedia has more than seven years' experience in producing website solutions for its clients. These include both database-driven (or dynamic) websites and content management systems (CMS).

On a database-driven (dynamic) website, all or part of the content is stored in a database rather than being normal, static HTML (HyperText Markup Language) pages. When a visitor goes to a dynamic page, the information is pulled from the database and displayed to the user at that moment. As long as the database is up to date, the user will always view the latest information. Most websites that contain many pages in the same format, such as product pages in an e-commerce site, are database-driven.

It is not only large sites that benefit from being database-driven. Many smaller sites contain an area that would benefit from being updateable in-house, such as a 'latest news' or 'events' section, an email newsletter, a members-only area, a search facility, downloadable documents or even just the text on the homepage. Having a website where content is updated regularly can encourage visitors to return more frequently, whereas content that is clearly out of date will discourage repeat visitors.

A CMS is an administration area that allows the website to be updated directly by the website owner/administrator. This is done through a normal web browser and is an easy-to-use, form-based system that requires no specialist knowledge. Most CMSs are linked to a database, so as a result they can also have dynamic content. The areas that most benefit from a CMS are those that change frequently, such as product details or categories for an online catalogue/e-commerce site, news section that contains date-dependent actions, and downloadable assets such as a monthly brochure in PDF (portable document format) format.

One of the advantages of the CMS is that it is a bespoke solution that can be tailored to each project. The extent of the content that needs to be updated in-house changes from project to project, so an off-the-shelf solution to content management may be unnecessarily expensive or not flexible enough to fulfil a client's requirements.

Web designers work in every industry. They may be employed directly by an organisation as part of the IT team, or they may work for IT consultancies or dedicated web design agencies. This is also an area where there are plenty of opportunities for freelancers.

Many web designers multi-task and would be better described as 'website developers'. They are not only responsible for the appearance and 'feel' of a website, but they also do the coding, pilot the site and maintain it for their clients after its launch. They need a high degree of creativity – websites need to be attention-grabbing as well as user-friendly – and need to be skilled programmers.

Typically, developing and launching a website will involve the following stages.

- The client has some ideas about what they want their website to do – publicise their services, offer a purchasing option, host a chat facility, etc. – and who it is intended to appeal to. They discuss their ideas with the designer, who should be able to contribute suggestions about the site's functionality (how it will operate) and its appearance.

- The client and designer will establish boundaries in terms of budget and time constraints. A designer may have ideas for an all-singing, all-dancing website – but if the client only has £1,000 to spend and needs the site up and running by the end of the month, those ideas will be useless.

- The designer and client will identify and source the content for the website. Some designers offer a comprehensive service that includes writing copy and providing illustrations. Others will outsource these tasks – or get the client to provide the required content.

- The designer will write the programming code for the website. This may involve starting from scratch or the adaptation of an existing site.

- Once the website is complete, it will need to be tested and piloted to make sure it meets the client's requirements. At this point, any technical problems can be ironed out.

- Finally the website will be uploaded onto a server and registered with different search engines.

If a website designer works for a small consultancy or as a freelance, they'll be responsible for fulfilling all these stages in the process. In larger companies, there may be dedicated account managers and programmers, so the designer can focus more on the creative aspects of the work.

Helen Butt runs Labrys Multimedia. Here she talks about her career and the type of work that she's involved in.

'I have a BA (Hons) in Communication Arts and English. Initially I planned to be a TV producer, but when I graduated I was offered a job at Huddersfield University to research how businesses could exploit multimedia. At that point the Internet had just been invented and the whole idea of communicating or selling products and services online was in its infancy. I got involved in setting up a commercial multimedia unit at the university and worked as a project manager, mainly developing multimedia CD-ROMs. I hadn't planned to work in the Web but I was lucky to have the opportunity to work in an exciting new field. I found that I enjoyed the challenges and that I had an eye for design and enjoyed the creative process.

'After about four years, I left to set up my own business and to work in partnership with the programmer I still work with now. A couple of years ago, I took a year off to travel. Since I came back, I've continued working as a multimedia designer and producer, specialising in educational resources.

'I design and build websites and other interactive multimedia resources. Most of my work is generated by word of mouth and I have several longstanding clients that I work with regularly. My contribution to individual projects varies enormously, and I'm often involved from inception through to their publication on the Internet. Sometimes a project needs specialist programming, and then I work in collaboration with a programmer with whom I have a longstanding professional relationship. On other occasions I'm part of a flexible production team, which can include writers, programmers and print-based designers.

'I operate as a sole trader and work from my office at home. Business and management skills are important, even for a lone worker in this field. It's essential that I keep clear records of business transactions for tax returns, etc. I also have to manage my time effectively and communicate effectively with a range of clients and colleagues.

'I recently tendered for, and won, a job developing the Independent Domestic Abuse Service (IDAS) website and redesigning their branding. I have quite a lot of experience in working for not-for-profit organisations so I understand that type of organisation's needs and I can keep costs low. They wanted a complete rebrand because the organisation had changed its name and developed its scope. They also wanted to develop a website aimed at professional and service users, including young people.

'The first stage was to hold initial meetings with the client to explore their needs and understand their target audience. During these initial meetings, I was also able to explore design ideas with them and learn more about the information and messages they needed to convey.

'I developed a site plan for the website so IDAS understood what information they needed to supply, and could spot gaps in this information. At the same time, I supplied three sample design ideas for their logo and business stationery.

'When IDAS approved the logo, I developed a homepage design to show them how information would be presented, then began to build webpage templates and input information into these templates. Throughout the website build, the client had access to a development area where they could monitor the progress of the website and suggest content amendments or revisions. The website was launched at a special event and it has received very positive feedback from stakeholders and service users.

'I used Adobe Illustrator to develop logo ideas and to draw illustrations, Adobe Photoshop to create webpage design and Adobe DreamWeaver to build the HTML template and CSS stylesheets. 'The Den' – a web area aimed at younger children – was built using Adobe Flash to provide a higher level of animation and interaction. The dynamic elements of the website, including the content management system, were written in ASP by my programming colleague.

'Like every career, there are pros and cons. I enjoy the creative process of creating a design from scratch, interpreting clients' ideas and helping to realise them. And I love the independence of being my own boss, and the variety of the workload. At the same time, there's the inevitable instability of income that all self-employed people experience, and sometimes the long periods of isolation can be difficult.

'To succeed in this field, I think you need a number of different attributes and skills. Obviously, creativity is important, but you also have to be able to communicate well with other people, particularly when it comes to interpreting clients' ideas and needs. The ability to organise vast arrays of information into a coherent design and structure is essential, and you have to pay attention to detail. I'd also say that you need good literacy skills so you can respond to briefs and write proposals, the ability to understand the needs of different target audiences – and tenacity.'

GAMES DESIGN

The interactive games industry is huge. New games may cost millions of pounds and involve a lot of people to develop – but if they catch the public imagination, they can generate massive returns on the initial investment.

Production studios, or large organisations that want to create spin-offs from other products, may commission new games. Alternatively, developers themselves may come up with concepts and pitch these to potential clients, who will finance their development. Companies that specialise in games design and production vary enormously in size: the largest employ hundreds of staff, but there are also a lot of small independent studios with fewer than five personnel. These will outsource elements of the game development that they can't complete themselves (such as artwork, animation and design and graphics) to specialist companies or freelancers.

After coming up with an initial idea for a game, developers will produce design documents that determine the elements that make up the final product. At this point, they often create a storyboard and script, and also establish the mechanics of the game. The next stage is to decide the technical aspects of the game and create the game codes, animation, graphics, audio production and special effects. Because so much work is involved, games designers often work in teams that combine a range of expertise.

The work of individual games designers varies. Some may be in at the concept stage; others will be brought in when the initial ideas are in place. Their role is to plan and define the elements and components of a game, such as its setting, rules, story, characters, etc. Their work will usually be strictly controlled by time and budgetary constraints, so they don't have a totally free hand to design whatever they want. Their work will be passed on to the technical team that does the actual programming. Games designers will also work with games testers when the prototypes come out so that they can identify modifications if they are required.

Because developing top-of-the-range computer games can cost millions of pounds, companies will lose a lot of money if the game doesn't grab audiences, or worse still doesn't work properly. Before a game goes public, the games testers look for problems such as program bugs, audio and graphical glitches, or spelling mistakes.

MULTIMEDIA DESIGN

As well as designing websites, Labrys Multimedia produces CD-ROMs in Adobe Director. Their work has included educational and training material, presentations and sales tools, and children's games. They use Director's programming language, Lingo, to develop applications that require a high level of interactivity.

An example of their work in this field is Making Better Places, a learning package that focuses on the development of design and the built environment for students aged 16–19. Labrys designed and built a website for the project and an accompanying CD-ROM to deliver the learning materials. Both resources include clickable maps with accompanying MPEG video clips, PowerPoint presentations, games and PDFs to support classroom teaching.

For this particular job, Labrys worked with an educational resource provider that carried out the project management and liaised with the client, but for many of their contracts they handle all stages from project management through to design and programming.

One of the key skills required in this type of work is a problem-solving approach. What does the client really need? A website or a CD-ROM? Which solution will deliver the best result and be most cost-effective? Because technology is a closed book to many people, the multimedia designer needs to be able to explain complicated concepts simply and give sound advice. The client may well be relying on them, because they don't understand what multimedia platforms can deliver.

WHAT DOES IT TAKE TO SUCCEED?

Ideally, an interactive media designer will:

- be enthusiastic about technology – you need to love the stuff to work with it all the time

- be logical and totally in love with problem-solving

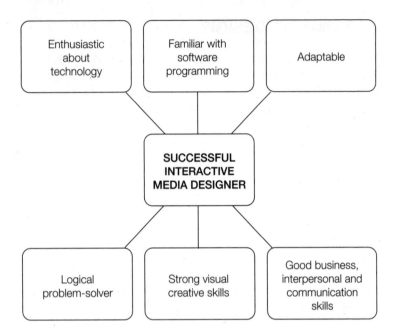

- be familiar with the principles of software programming

- have strong visual creative skills – at the end of the day you have to design something that will appeal to your audience

- be adaptable – software develops all the time and you'll need to pick up new techniques and keep up with changes in the industry. You may also be expected to multi-task within your own company. This isn't an industry that stands still and the job that you do now may well not exist in 12 months' time. You need to be flexible, to be prepared to move around from company to company to broaden your experience and to change career direction if necessary

- have strong interpersonal, business and communication skills so that you can interpret your clients' needs – you are unlikely to have a free hand and unlimited budget to design a website, so you need an awareness of how business operates. You may be expected to create budgets, manage your own and other staff's time, negotiate with clients and give presentations on a regular basis.

Specialist technical skills are essential. You'll need to understand how software and hardware work, even if you're not actually programming. Every system has capabilities and constraints that will influence your designs, so you'll have to be aware of these. Expect to acquire knowledge about multimedia design theory, the principles of software programming, information and systems architecture, user-centred design, and audio, visual and graphic design. Although this sounds quite daunting on paper, if you're enthusiastic about interactive media, you'll already be familiar with many of the principles because they underpin a lot of the things you use every day.

Essential skills

As well as specialist and general skills, practitioners working in interactive media or computer games need an all-round awareness of the industry, its processes and business issues as a whole. Successful practitioners need to be self-motivated and autonomous, and have an entrepreneurial attitude and a willingness to continue learning. They must have a broad outlook and be willing to embrace … cross-disciplinary roles. A lack of this general awareness is considered detrimental to the functioning of companies as it affects communication and productivity. An example of this can be seen in the production process, which is not a simple production line, where each person can complete his or her task and hand over to the next. Each individual needs an awareness of the wider process and their place within it, so that they can ensure their work is not just finished, but also ready for the next person. Designers need to appreciate technical and business issues; programmers need to have design awareness; managers need to understand creative processes and technical constraints and, most importantly, all must understand the needs of end-users.

(Source: 'National Occupation Standards: Interactive Media' available from www.skillset.org)

This is also a profession that demands a high degree of discipline. You may be required to work to tight deadlines which are non-negotiable; if your client has committed to launch a website by a certain date, you'll need to deliver it. Discipline is particularly important if you are freelance and work alone or in a small team, where there is nobody to manage your performance. Maintaining the degree of concentration and precision to develop and program a site is not an easy task, particularly if you are working long hours.

If you're planning to be a games designer, you should already be passionate about interactive games – only experienced players understand what really makes them work. You'll need a thorough understanding of game-play theory, and good storytelling and narrative development skills. You'll also have to be happy working in a team because games are usually developed by a number of people collaborating closely. You'll work to tight deadlines and have to understand production and marketing schedules.

STARTING YOUR CAREER

The workforce in the interactive media industry is highly qualified. Most practitioners have graduate, and many have postgraduate, qualifications. Yes, it's possible that your experience of designing websites for your friends will get you a job in an agency – but increasingly employers expect new recruits to have appropriate technical and professional qualifications, usually to degree level (or equivalent).

There are a number of educational routes that you can follow, so before you choose a course it's worth doing your homework.

■ At degree level, you can study a range of courses in IT, computer science and software engineering. Course content varies enormously, so you need to examine them carefully to find one that plays to both your interests and strengths. Alternatively, you may want to follow a more traditional academic course such as maths or physics; these can also provide a useful starting point for a career in web design. You'll need at least two relevant A-levels to apply, and courses usually last three or four years; check whether they include periods of work experience, which can be a valuable addition to your CV when you start looking for a job.

- Alternatively you can opt for a qualification that offers more specialist training in web design, interactive design and IT, such as the two-year, full-time BTEC National Diploma in Art and Design (Multimedia), Computer Studies or IT. You'll normally need a minimum of four GCSEs or equivalent to qualify.

- BTEC Higher National Diplomas may be offered on a full- or part-time basis, or as sandwich courses combined with work experience. You will usually need a minimum of one A-level and four GCSEs (or equivalent) to apply.

- If you're already working in a relevant field, you can study for an NVQ/SVQ, which will give you a relevant qualification either by day release or distance learning.

- If you're still in full-time education and don't want to go to university, keep an eye open for apprenticeships in IT. The number of these – and the areas that they are available in – varies from year to year depending on government initiatives and the state of the employment market. Check out the opportunities on www. apprenticeships.org.uk

If your particular interest is games design, and you decide to follow a dedicated course, check out its content carefully before you commit. Does it offer a balance between programming, game art and game design? The University of Abertay, Dundee, University of the West of Scotland, and Glamorgan Centre for Design and Technology all offer courses that specialise in computer games technology.

Course info

BA Honours Animation at Middlesex is an exciting new programme reflecting the amazing technological times in which we live. Animation was once limited to cinema and television, but now has many new platforms including web design, electronic street advertising and mobile phone visual ring tones. Animation at Middlesex is a gateway into this vibrant ever-changing creative industry. You will be encouraged to find your own voice as a filmmaker and develop original and innovative approaches, whilst gaining a solid grounding in all aspects of contemporary animation production. You will learn 3D CGI, 2D digital, stop motion, as well as exploring classical 2D and experimental animation techniques. You'll be taught all the technical, design and cognitive skills necessary to establish yourself in today's highly competitive and exciting animation industry or alternatively to move on to postgraduate study.

(Source: www.mdx.ac.uk)

Once you're established in a job, you'll need to keep up with new developments in the industry; this isn't a discipline where you learn your trade and you're established for life. Check out the website of the British Computer Society (www.bcs.org) to find out what professional qualifications are available.

So far we've focused on moving into interactive design via qualifications and training in IT-related subjects. There is another route: some web designers have started from a traditional art and design background. Designers in all fields work with technology and some have crossed over from their original discipline into web design, combining their creative talent with technical expertise to forge new careers.

As your career develops, you may find that you move into a particular field such as education and learning website design, customer service, market research, etc. This specialisation can be valuable if you decide to work freelance or set up your own agency. If you are known, for example,

Junior to Mid-weight Front End Web Developer

Salary £25K + benefits. We have a longstanding relationship with nearly all our clients. We design, build and maintain their sites and, in most cases, we host the sites for them too, as they use our content management and online communications tools. We also provide consultancy services, as well as other corporate communications projects such as mobile sites and online reporting. The kind of skills that you will need in order to work on our clients' projects include: (X)HTML, CSS, ASP. Some experience of the following would prove beneficial: Javascript, Flash Actionscript, Coldfusion.

as a talented designer of websites for authors, your name will get passed around.

What are future prospects like for interactive media designers? Helen Butt says:

> I think that the demand for designers will decrease in the short term, particularly in the commercial sector. However, there'll always be a drive to ensure that information is communicated effectively and that web designs are commercially appealing, so in the longer term there will always be a healthy demand for skilled and talented designers.

◉ Take action

- If you've read through this chapter in its entirety, you probably already have an interest in this discipline and some idea of what areas you're likely to go into. Keep up to date with changes in the technology for your chosen field – it is constantly being upgraded.

- Read professional magazines regularly – it's another way to keep abreast of changes in the industry.

■ Check out company websites to see how they work. Look for design trends. Can you see particular styles and design motifs that are favoured by particular industries? What about the public sector – what sort of image are its organisations trying to cultivate?

■ If you have the expertise, volunteer your services to friends and acquaintances who might want a website developing. Even if you do the work for free, it's valuable experience.

■ Your technical services will be much appreciated by charities and voluntary organisations, so get involved – once again, it will give you good experience and contribute to your CV and portfolio.

Chapter Eight
INTERIOR DESIGN

Interior designers plan the design of living and commercial environments. The scope of their work varies enormously. A millionaire moving into a mansion in Mayfair will think nothing about paying a reputable interior design agency a few hundred thousand pounds to design a 'look' for her new home, advise on structural alterations and project-manage a two-year redevelopment. At the other end of the scale, a homeowner who recognises his own lack of aptitude in this field may hire a local designer for a couple of hundred pounds to come in for an afternoon and advise them on colour schemes and soft furnishings for the bedroom.

Obviously, interior designers are not just concerned with redesigning domestic environments. Some specialise in offices, others in pub or bar design. Some work exclusively on new-builds, others focus on historic buildings. This is one area where, with application, dedication and a bit of luck, you can specialise in an area that really appeals to you.

There are between 6,000 and 8,000 interior designers in the UK, working in design consultancies, architectural practices or as freelance, self-employed consultants. Some have branched out into highly lucrative sidelines including journalism (the thirst for glossy interior design magazines shows no signs of abating) or setting up retail outlets for products related to their trade.

It's important to be realistic about what the work involves. Only those at the very top of the profession can sweep into a venue *à la* Lawrence Llewellyn-Bowen and design according to their own whims. Most interior designers will respond to a brief from their clients, and be restricted in what they can achieve by budgets and time constraints.

What is an interior designer?

The British Interior Design Association (BIDA) defines interior designers as people who are 'qualified by training and experience to plan the design and execution of interior projects and their furnishings, and to organise the various arts and crafts essential to their completion. A designer is one who identifies, researches and creatively solves problems pertaining to the function and quality of the interior environment... provides a full consultancy service including programming, design analysis, space planning, aesthetics, monitoring work on site, using specialised knowledge of interior construction, building systems and components, building regulations, equipment, materials and furnishings; and prepares drawings and documents relative to the design of interior space.'

(www.bida.org)

WHAT DOES IT TAKE TO SUCCEED?

My passion for interior design started when I was very young – my mother was very talented in creating different looks around the home, and she often helped friends when they were redesigning rooms, so I absorbed her interest. She taught me a lot about colour and using space.

(Sally Smith, interior designer)

As with most careers in the design industry, you need an aptitude for, and a genuine interest in, interior design before you start exploring educational and professional opportunities. This is a highly competitive field and there is simply no point in 'playing' at it. If you're going to build a career and make a reasonable living, you'll need a lot of talent, even more dedication – and probably a bit of luck to get you started.

It's important to accept that not all of us have these talents. We can learn the theory of interior design but that doesn't mean that we can put together a stylish

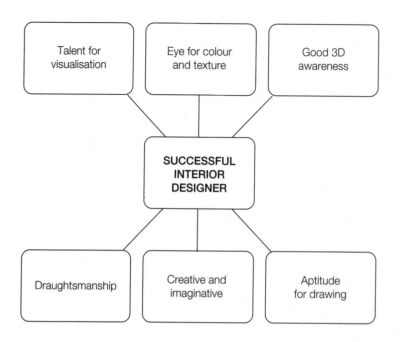

interior. It's no different to the way that many of us can learn musical notation but still can't get anything more than a howl like a strangled cat from a violin. Some people have an 'eye' for design; the rest of us need help. If you're one of the latter, choose a different career path. No amount of tuition is going to give you the talent that a successful designer needs to display.

In an interview with the *Guardian* in May 2007, interior designer Anthony Brewster said:

> I think the main interest for someone who wants to work in design should be a desire to make beautiful environments for people to live and work in. Finding the solution that you have been looking for or struggling to find is an awesome feeling… If you want to work in interior design you need to become a sponge. You never know until the time comes how much you have picked up, so simply put yourself in the position to see and hear about design and you will suck up more knowledge than you realise.

In practical terms, if you're planning a career as an interior designer you'll need a number of technical, business and interpersonal skills. Yes, it's great that your friends think you have a good eye for colour and you can put together a mood board, but you may also have to:

- inspect and carry out preliminary surveys on buildings – that means understanding the technicalities of the building trade. Advising a client to create an open, light living space by taking down a weight-bearing wall isn't a good idea

- research materials and costs, and balance budgets – you'll be expected to prepare plans (and you may also be purchasing materials) that your client is happy to pay for. Creating the ultimate dream kitchen with £1,000-a-metre granite work surface, handmade cupboards and the latest Smeg fittings isn't appropriate if your client is on a flat-pack budget

- draw up rough and detailed designs for client approval – most designers use sophisticated computer-aided design (CAD) software and/or models to show clients what the final outcome will be – so computer and technical literacy is essential

- supervise a wide range of contractors to make sure they work to schedule (a notoriously difficult task) – you could be working with architects, local council officials, builders, engineers, surveyors, furniture manufacturers, decorators… Bringing together these diverse people, who all have other commitments that will undoubtedly clash with your schedule, demands diplomacy and authority.

Interior design is a fascinating – and potentially rewarding – career, but don't make the mistake of thinking it's an easy option. If you work for a successful consultancy or establish your own business, you may have to work long and irregular hours. You're moving into a profession that is ruled by financial and time restraints and deadlines that you'll be expected to meet. Although your job may be 9 am to 5 pm on paper, expect to work late nights and weekends if the job demands it.

Many designers spend a lot of their time on the road, pitching for work, visiting clients, sourcing materials and supervising contractors. You may be office-based but you could spend a fair amount of time in your car.

You'll also have to spend time upgrading your skills and knowledge. Design trends change continually – and you'll be expected to keep up. You will need to constantly update your technical skills to meet the demands of new developments in CAD. If your design skills are excellent but your presentation and business skills are lousy, you may need additional professional training in these areas. You'll certainly need to visit exhibitions, read around the subject and talk to the people who influence the business. You'll do all of this in your own time.

A day in the life of Sally Smith, interior designer

case STUDY

There's no such thing as a typical day – one of the great things about this job is the variety. The hours are unpredictable because I work for myself and I need to make the most of every job that comes in. Sometimes I'll have a spell of nine to five, but if I'm in the middle of a project, I'll start much earlier and work late. Plus, I have to make time to see clients and, if I'm working on an interior with a client who is out all day, I may have to meet them in the evening.

My first job when I get into my studio in the morning is to check emails, and follow up any new leads. Sometimes that can be frustrating, particularly if I'm in the middle of a project that's really absorbing. But if the business is going to continue, I have to line up more work and I can't afford to miss a lead. Administration takes up about a third of my time. I try to keep up with my accounts and marketing on a regular basis, because there's nothing worse than coming to the end of the financial year with no paperwork ready for your accountant.

I work with a loose network of other people so that if there's a job I need help with there's always someone to call in. I specialise in domestic interiors, but occasionally I've been asked to pitch for commercial work. When that happens, I work with a couple of colleagues who have a lot of experience in that field. On a collaborative project like that, we have regular team meetings to discuss progress and check that everyone is up to speed. Meeting deadlines and cost control are important parts of the job, so it's essential that we're all in regular contact.

The rest of my day may be spent meeting clients, chasing up new leads, or working in the studio on a particular design project. I could be creating mood boards, drafting designs either by sketching or using CAD. I still like to plan my work using pencil and paper – I find that it gives me more freedom – but like everyone else I use software to create designs and plans.

When I'm in the middle of a project, I spend a lot of time on site overseeing the work. That's not essential – some interior designers use specialist project managers once the designs have been agreed. My projects tend to be smaller and I like to be involved, so I'll work directly with the decorators, carpenters, upholsterers, etc. Over the years I've built up a team of tradespeople that I know I can rely on and they don't seem to mind me poking my nose in!

I'm passionate about my work so I'm happy to put in the hard work that's required. And it is hard – I get annoyed sometimes by articles in the media that give the impression that this is a glorified hobby or a job for dilettantes! Like any other profession, it demands dedication, attention to detail and continual application. As well as doing my job, I also have to keep up with new trends so I never really stop. Even on holiday, I'll find myself looking at interiors and thinking, 'Now, how would that work…?'

STARTING YOUR CAREER

Some individuals like Sally Smith have morphed very successfully into interior designers. Their aptitude in transforming living or commercial spaces for themselves and their friends has been recognised on a wider scale and they've developed a business.

Sally is self-taught. She worked in numerous retail outlets that specialised in furniture and soft furnishings, had a spell working for an estate agent which gave her a lot of basic knowledge about domestic buildings, and studied in her spare time to get the technical design skills she needed. That, combined with her natural flair, has enabled her to start her own business.

Increasingly, however, young interior designers are pursuing a formal educational path into the profession, studying for a degree or HND in interior design or a related design or architecture subject. If you're planning to follow this route, do your research and look for a course that meets your needs and those of the professional associations that regulate the profession.

BIDA states that a professional-level interior design course should encompass the following areas:

1   *Fundamentals of design (philosophy, sociology, aesthetics and a theory of design). Visual research (colour, light, form, texture). Basic knowledge of materials.*

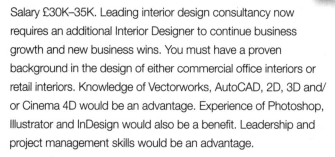

Interior Designer

Salary £30K–35K. Leading interior design consultancy now requires an additional Interior Designer to continue business growth and new business wins. You must have a proven background in the design of either commercial office interiors or retail interiors. Knowledge of Vectorworks, AutoCAD, 2D, 3D and/ or Cinema 4D would be an advantage. Experience of Photoshop, Illustrator and InDesign would also be a benefit. Leadership and project management skills would be an advantage.

2   Visual communication (objective and interpretative drawing, freehand perspective drawing, use of colour media, photography and model making).

3   People in their environment (human ergonometric and anthropometric studies and people in space and design evaluation). History of art and architecture, interiors and furniture.

4   Creative work by project method.

5   Interpretation of the project schemes and technical studies related to the built environment (working drawings, building technology, and understanding of structure and services. Costing and estimating, detailing and specifying material, furniture and fittings).

6   Professional practice (verbal communication techniques, office organisation and practice, legislation affecting the designer, visiting projects underway or completed).

(Source: www.bida.org)

Distance learning courses in interior design are advertised in the back of lifestyle magazines. Be wary of courses that promise to fully train you in six months and are not affiliated to, or accredited by, reputable educational organisations. If you are planning a serious career as an interior designer, your course must be recognised as providing a high standard of education and training.

If you're completely new to this discipline, you could find it useful to study for a National Certificate in Further Education, which can be completed at adult evening classes, or an access to interior design course: a one-year, full-time course for entrants with few formal qualifications or mature students.

The range of available courses can appear confusing, so you'll need advice to choose wisely. You could choose a three-year, full-time degree course in interior and special design or a foundation degree in interior design that will last for two years, full-time, and include 16 weeks' work experience. Alternatively, there are a number of colleges offering an HND in interior design that you can study part-time, or by distance learning if you are already employed.

What does an undergraduate degree course in interior design involve?

This is an extract from the prospectus of University College Falmouth:

> *With an emphasis on professional practice, Interior Design is about maximising potential, transforming spaces through working with clients and other specialists, to develop innovative and creative design solutions. From exploring the fundamentals of materials and structure to planning and creating exciting interior spaces, you'll cover every aspect of interior Design. You'll not only learn about the construction and detailing of space, and how to communicate your designs to professional standards through traditional and digital presentation techniques, you'll also be given the inspiration and encouragement to find your own personal approach to interior Design.*
>
> *As with most careers, education is a great help but it doesn't replace practical experience. You need on-the-job training and a chance to hone your skills.*
>
> *(www.falmouth.ac.uk)*

Students on this course work with experienced architects, landscape architects and interior designers on live projects, designing for a range of commercial users, including hospitality, retail, public, marine and leisure. They also learn how professional Interior Design interacts with other disciplines and develop valuable project management skills.

Many students complete a first degree in another subject, such as architecture, then follow a postgraduate course in interior design. The MA Interior Design programme at the University of Central Lancashire has been running for a number of years. The course encourages students to follow their own interests and to complete a body of work to a professional standard. At the same time, they carry out research and field practice and learn more about the principles of professional interior design practice.

Occasionally, established consultancies will offer trainee posts to a candidate who hasn't got a degree or diploma. Because these opportunities are so few and far between, competition for them is fierce and you'll be expected to prove that you have an aptitude for the discipline. That means presenting potential employers with a portfolio of designs that are appropriate to their business and that display your skills.

Ideally you'll also have some relevant experience through work placements or, if you're just leaving school, through the courses that you've studied. Don't dismiss openings in seemingly unrelated work areas. Working as a volunteer in a charity shop could give you valuable insight into display work. A weekend or vacation job in a furniture or DIY store will help you to acquire both customer service skills and an insight into trends and fashions in domestic interior design.

You'll also impress employers if you have at least some familiarity with relevant computer design software. Although you may not be able to get hands-on experience in using particular packages, you can research their capability via the Internet.

Interior Designer

Salary to £40K. Due to continued business growth, one of the most high-tech and forward-thinking commercial interior fit-out specialists now needs an experienced Interior Designer to work on commercial office interiors. You should be an experienced interior designer, accustomed to working on projects from concepts through to detailed drawings. You should be fully literate in all main CAD software, and 3D modelling/rendering as well as space planning and structural work. Ideally you'll be used to meeting with clients, have top-class presentation skills and a modern approach to your work. You should also have project management skills and be used to liaising with architects and contractors, etc.

Vacancies for interior designers will be publicised in trade publications, such as *Design Week* and *Architects' Journal*, but you will find more opportunities online.

www.creativepool.co.uk offers a platform for recruiters and employers of interior designers to advertise vacancies, and for practitioners to publicise their expertise.

www.design4design.com is an online resource centre for architects and designers offering information on jobs, courses, products, books and magazines.

❷ Take action

- Start reading around the subject. Source magazines and books from your local library to learn more about current trends in interior design.

- Enter 'professional+interior+designers' on your Internet search engine and explore websites for some of the larger organisations. What sort of influences can you identify in their work?

- Don't restrict yourself to one area of the discipline – remember that there are more jobs for people in the commercial sector than in designing domestic interiors.

- Start making up mood boards and designs for friends and family. The more you can practise your skills, the better.

- Talk to an interior designer to get their take on the profession. There are plenty of consultancies across the country – if you don't know any designers yourself, contact your local further education college and ask if they can put you in contact with someone.

Chapter Nine
BRAND DESIGN

Brand design involves determining all the factors that make a product or service (and the company that offers it) memorable to the people who use it. Brand designers may help to create everything from logos to packaging, staff uniforms to the colour scheme for the corporate HQ. There's a detailed explanation of brand design in Chapter 2.

THE POWER OF BRANDS

You want to buy a new car/pair of trainers/can of baked beans/perfume. What influences your choice of purchase? Do you go for the cheapest – or do you opt for a brand that you trust? If you choose the latter, have you ever considered why you trust that brand? Is it the product itself that you particularly like – or are you influenced by the brand image?

Marketing experts have long understood that branding can ensure customer loyalty – and in a competitive global marketplace, that is worth an awful lot of money. We often assume that branding only applies to heavily promoted, mass-consumer goods but, in fact, almost everything has a brand. Organisations in both the public and private sectors have brands of some sort – even if it's only the company or department name. So, as well as Apple, we have JobCentre; as well as Coca-Cola, we have the Open University. Those names act as shorthand: they convey a wealth of connotations.

Brands are important because:

■ they are instantly recognisable

- they are a peg on which an organisation can hang a lot of positive information – the brand encompasses not only physical products and services, but also the organisation's values and personality

- they can create a sense of belonging among users

- they can deter competitors – if your product or service becomes the brand leader, it will be hard to replace; Pepsi has been trying to push Coca-Cola from the top of the soft drink brand tree for years without success.

Understanding the psychology of purchasing and the techniques of marketing are essential for anyone who wants to go into brand development and design. You have to know what attracts people to a product or service and what keeps their interest. You have to accept that the product or service itself is eventually secondary to the brand image. Coca-Cola is, after all, nothing more than flavoured water, but its name, bottle shape, use of colour, image and music in its advertising and promotion has made it so much more.

The value of branding in today's competitive global environment has increased as organisations continue to compete in overcrowded markets. As consumers become more sophisticated and the plethora of products more similar, the need to differentiate through emotional attachment has become an ever-increasing need. The key to successful brand development is an understanding of its synergistic relationship with innovation. The popular view has been that branding is connected with logos, advertising and manipulation, while innovation is to do with more process-orientated development. We believe that these viewpoints are mistaken. For us, branding is about delivering a rewarding experience to customers, while innovation is about an organisational effort aimed at differentiating a company through original value creation. In other words, each is inextricably linked.

(Source: University of the Creative Arts)

Ian Loseby, who founded successful brand design company Arris, believes that branding is essential in helping people to understand the culture, values and appeal of a company. 'It's a visual marker that uses tremendously powerful symbolism. If I said "stars and stripes" you'd say "America". If I showed a picture of an American flag to 30 people, what would they think about it? The response would be massive. You can apply the same principle to a company brand.'

Over the last 16 years, Ian's company has provided high-profile branding for all types of businesses, from FTSE 100s to local small enterprises. He believes that, essentially, branding is a very simple concept that some people try to turn into an art form. 'Everything we do is about solving problems and understanding what people want. My service has expanded from just creating materials that communicate to advising on, and supplying, the best types of media, the best materials, the best marketing channels. We help clients to add value and be more cost-effective.'

Jonathan Armstead of bluestone design agrees:

> When clients are boxed into a corner, we give them a solution. That might initially be for a specific part of their business, but from that we can advise on other areas. So, for example, we might start by helping with corporate publications, then help with direct mail campaigns and organise displays at exhibitions for them. By working across the board, we're helping their brand gain consistency – and that's essential if a brand is going to be recognised.

Designers use problem-solving skills to connect with their client's customers, constituencies or communities. This is particularly important when the global market has stimulated such high levels of competition and when many companies, brands and institutions are struggling to maintain their appeal. It doesn't take much to damage a brand: allegations of using overly cheap labour were enough to damage Primark's reputation. Design can play a central role in helping brands to reposition themselves so that more people trust them.

Jonathan Armstead founded bluestone design in 1998 and is managing director of the company, whose clients include Morrisons, Alton Towers and Alpha BT.

Like many designers, he works across a number of disciplines – you will already have met him if you read the chapter on exhibition design, another area in which his company specialises.

'We specialise in creative branding solutions – we're a multi-disciplined company that helps clients connect with their various audiences. We can help them with every aspect of their brand – advertising, digital media, direct mail, exhibitions, identity, public relations, packaging, web design. So, for example, when we worked to rebrand a market leader in lifestyle homes and investment opportunities in Austria, we created a new corporate ID, advertising and a website. With a country clothing boutique, we designed their logo, stationery, signage, window graphics, labels, invitations and bags, advertising and brochureware. We were able to give them a level of brand consistency that they wouldn't have got if they'd used an agency with a more limited offer.

'There are four other staff – two designers, a company secretary, and an account handler. I've deliberately kept the team small and maintained the business as an independent agency. I've thought about expanding the team but our system works well – we win business because of our creativity. Once we're working on a commission, we entrust work to people we've worked with and marry the right people to the right part of the job. So, we have a network of first-rate copywriters, illustrators, web designers, etc. that we can call on. Working this way keeps the costs clear and the client knows what they're paying for, so that makes them happy. They pay for what they use, not the wages of a large number of bluestone staff.

'Our design is functional and affordable – at the end of the day, it always comes down to cost. We can offer any service that a client requires, from overseeing new brand development, to producing corporate literature, web design and exhibitions. We give them solutions and we help them recognise their strengths.

'Ultimately, whether they are multi-million-pound organisations or small businesses, the clients are looking for help but it's often for more than one aspect of their business. We can give them the solutions they need.'

CREATING AND DEVELOPING A BRAND

Brand design is sometimes known as 'experience design'. In Ralph Ardill's essay for the Design Council, 'Introduction to experience design', he states:

> *Experience design concentrates on moments of engagement between people and brands, and the memories these moments create. For customers, all these moments of corporate experience combine to shape perceptions, motivate their brand commitment and influence the likelihood of repurchase in the future. Experience design is not driven by a single design discipline but instead requires a truly cross-discipline perspective that considers all aspects of the brand/business – from product, packaging and retail environment to the clothing and attitude of employees.*

So what is involved in creating and developing a brand or an experience? First, the design company needs to do its research and find out about the characteristics of the industry their client operates in. What does that industry do? What challenges and opportunities does it face? Who are the client's main competitors? How is the client company currently positioned – does it need to change its position gradually or try to achieve a higher profile in a very short period of time?

The next step would be to analyse the client's qualities and values and consider how they can be used to rebrand. Can the existing brand be adjusted – or is a whole new approach needed? It's important to consider how the public will perceive a rebranding exercise. If an organisation is experiencing a downturn and share values are falling, its stakeholders may not appreciate £100,000 being spent on a new image. Rebranding should never be done for its own sake – it has to have a clear purpose and it must lead to a better understanding of the client's business.

It's essential, therefore, to examine the target audience. What will appeal to the organisation's customers and consumers? What will turn them away? What triggers will they respond to? Once the designers understand this, they can formulate targeted messages and identify key marketing channels that will help the client to acquire new customers and retain existing ones. These messages can be developed into elements of marketing campaigns that combine ideas, words and images.

The advantage of using a brand designer to do this as opposed to using different design agencies for different parts of the work is that the client can achieve consistency. The same messages can be communicated across the client company, from its stationery, to its logo, to its website, to its corporate uniform, to its direct mail… The brand designer can think holistically, consider how the different parts of the client company can be unified and create a unified, memorable image.

As Ian Loseby says:

> You have to understand your customer: do they want to stand out or do they want to follow current trends? Some smaller companies want to look like the bigger companies, they want to fit in and if you make them stand out, they won't appreciate it. There's no point in putting a shy person in the middle of the room with a spotlight on them; they're just not going to respond. But the showman, who wants something different, wants the spotlight.

The larger brand design agencies will also offer training to their clients' employees so that everyone in the company knows what the company is about. As Ralph Ardill points out:

> Companies are recognising the need for all of their people to 'live the brand' by developing internal programmes and culture change initiatives designed to turn strategic brand values into front-line behaviours. The design of such internal experience programmes and initiatives is likely to become a major growth area for experiential design.

WHAT DOES IT TAKE TO SUCCEED?

Brand designers need creative talent and an ability to look at the big picture rather than just focusing on a small aspect of design. They must appreciate how the various elements of a client's business fit together and complement each other. For that reason, as well as having a sharp eye for visual communications, brand designers need to have a feel for business.

Of all the design disciplines, this is the one that is most closely involved with marketing. Successful brand designers will understand the psychology of the marketplace, what makes customers choose one brand instead of another, what keeps them loyal – and what turns them off.

Branding can be an expensive exercise. If a new company decides that it wants a strong corporate identity that will feed through every aspect of its business, it will pay many thousands of pounds to achieve this. The results have to be right. If they're not, then the client loses money and also loses face when they have to rebrand in a short period of time after the initial exercise. Consequently clients can be demanding.

It's essential for brand designers to have vision and to be aware of what they can do with a brand, but at the same time they have to listen to their clients and understand what they want. Large companies often have large marketing departments and influential marketing managers who will have their own ideas about what the brand should involve. Clever designers find a way to work with the clients rather than trying to impose their own creativity. They'll manipulate and suggest rather than trying to steamroller their way through a commission.

As Ian Loseby says:

> *The person who's asking you to do a job usually has an idea of what they want – even if they don't tell you. The skill is in uncovering their thoughts and then ensuring you understand what they mean. You have to confirm and qualify what they mean all the time. I don't mind asking the obvious questions and requesting explanations. But the more influential the client, the more challenging I become, because they're often surrounded by people who say yes without understanding fully what is being asked. The client isn't always right, but they do hold the purse strings so you have to solve their problems and make them happy.*

Jonathan Armstead believes that good presentation skills are an integral part of his success in gaining commissions:

> *You have to be able to communicate with your client so they know that you understand them and their needs. You may have to explain some complex concepts when you're pitching for a job and you have to share your vision and explain why you've come up with a particular set of ideas. If they don't have confidence in you, you're not going to work well together.*

Management skills are also essential, particularly if you are working with a team of suppliers. Your clients will be working to strict budgets and deadlines and you'll have to be prepared to meet these.

Finally, you need to be in touch with ordinary people, not ensconced in a rarefied world of design specialists. Your job will be to connect with diverse audiences and to tap into the issues that they care about – whether this is sustainability, ethical production methods or keeping prices down. You can't do your job unless you keep your feet squarely on the ground.

So, the brand designer needs:

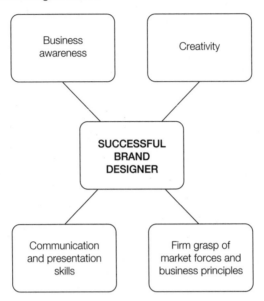

GETTING STARTED

It's most likely that you'll move into brand design from another design discipline, so you may have trained in graphic design or interactive media design. There are a few dedicated university courses in brand design management, but these are few and far between, often at postgraduate level or related to business or marketing modules.

If you're determined to go into this field, however, the University of the Creative Arts runs undergraduate courses in branding, marketing and advertising. But it is at master's level that you are most likely to find a relevant course. The School of Art and Design at Bath Spa University has an MA course in Brand Development that is open to candidates with degrees in any discipline. This aims to develop students' analytical, strategic and creative thinking processes together with the skills related to brand creation, identity, positioning and marketing.

Brunel University offers an MA in Design and Branding Strategy. The three-phase programme focuses on:

■ design research, creativity and innovation

- design management and marketing
- branding strategy.

The course highlights the range of issues that a brand designer needs to be aware of, including the influence of new technology, economics, social, environmental, sustainability on brands, research methods, the differences between consumer and industrial markets and the relationship of the brand and corporate strategy. Business awareness and the principles of marketing and consumerism are key features of courses like this.

At Brunel, students have to complete a dissertation to gain their MA. Examples of recent topics are: branding and national identity, luxury fashion branding and spiritual branding for boutique hotels.

As we've already stated, however, most brand designers will grow into their role having trained in alternative disciplines. You're more likely to move sideways into brand design, having started your career in a narrower role, for example, as a junior designer in an advertising or marketing company.

Competition for good jobs is strong. Design graduates will be competing with candidates from disciplines such as business management, advertising and PR who have a proven track record in developing brands. One possible career path is to work within the marketing function of a

Senior Brand Identity Designer

Salary £40K–50K. Outstanding brand creation design agency is looking for a lead designer to run a team, and add to their fantastic list of award-winning brand identities. The company is an amazing place to work with an atmosphere that encourages responsibility and superb creativity at every level. This is your chance to make an impact and expand your horizons. You must have branding experience that is second to none. You will have accolades that you enjoy boasting about and be inspiring in everything that you do.

large organisation; even if it contracts out its brand design work, you'll get a good grounding in the basic principles of the business.

One point to remember is that brand designers often spend very little time actually sitting at a computer or drawing board using their design skills. They are more likely to be in meetings with marketing managers examining ways in which the various facets of the brand can be stitched together, then briefing other designers on specific aspects of the job.

For the designers who make their mark and gain a reputation for successfully designing brands, the financial rewards can be very healthy.

This is also a discipline that is likely to continue growing in influence and size. Brands have become an integral part of our lives; in our minds we associate them not just with products but also with emotions such as trust and security. We build up relationships with brands – which explains why some of the most successful have survived for so long. Manufacturers and service providers are aware of this and are taking a much broader view of the way that they put their offers onto the open market and interact with their customers. Because of this, the demand for smart brand designers can only continue to rise.

@ Take action

- Start to study different brands to see how they work, and put together a brand scrapbook of your favourite examples.

- Read up on marketing and brand management. These are business concepts that you need to understand.

- Work on your own portfolio and make sure it is up to date. Remember that many brand designers have started as graphic designers, so look at relevant areas of skills development.

Chapter Ten
TRAINING, SKILLS AND QUALIFICATIONS

We live in a society that is obsessed with qualifications. The more cynical among us would argue that this is because they subscribe to the current passion for ticking boxes; when recruiters are looking for new staff they can use qualifications as a way to ensure that they get a certain type of applicant – and candidates have less chance of arguing that the process was unfair. The less cynical will tell you that the demand for qualifications reflects gains in educational achievement over the last few years: people are generally better educated and better qualified.

Whatever the reason, you'll find it difficult to get into a career in design without relevant qualifications and training, so in this chapter we'll look at some of the options that are available to you.

EDUCATIONAL QUALIFICATIONS

There are many different ways to study for qualifications in art and design. Your choice of pathway will depend on a number of factors:

- whether you would prefer to follow an academic or vocational course

- your age and existing educational qualifications

- your personal circumstances – can you afford full-time higher education?

- where you want to study.

Let's start by getting to grips with the various levels of qualification that are available.

Diplomas

If you're still at school and aged 14+, it's worth exploring the new Diploma in Creative and Media that has recently been introduced. The advantage of this type of course is that it will give you practical experience even though you'll continue to learn in the classroom. It will also give you useful background information and experience that relates to your chosen career.

The Diploma in Creative and Media looks at four areas of the creative process.

1   **Creativity in context**: the things that can influence the creative process, such as society, culture, the environment or the work of other people.

2   **Thinking and working creatively**: ways of exploring, experimenting with and developing ideas, skills and techniques.

3   **Principles, processes and practice**: the skills, techniques and processes to turn your ideas into reality.

4   **Creative businesses and enterprise**: an understanding of real situations and the skills that you need to succeed in the industry.

When you finish, you can progress to another course, such as A-level or NVQ. Alternatively, you can look for work or some form of apprenticeship. For a comprehensive introduction to Diplomas, plus case studies and a quiz, go to the government website, www.yp.direct.gov. uk/diplomas/

National Vocational Qualifications (NVQs)

National Vocational Qualifications (NVQs) are 'competence-based' qualifications that allow you to learn practical, work-related tasks that help you to develop the skills and knowledge to do a job effectively. They are based on national standards for various occupations. An NVQ could be appropriate if you already have skills and want to improve them, or if you are starting from scratch.

To study for an NVQ, you must have access to a working environment, either by working full- or part-time. You can study NVQs through college (and in some schools) or by distance learning. You'll be assessed on practical assignments and a portfolio of evidence. Normally, a qualified assessor will observe you and question you about the work you carry out in the workplace (or a realistic working environment) to test your knowledge and understanding as well as your actual performance.

Anyone considering a career in design who doesn't plan to follow a conventional design course might find some of the NVQs related to business and management, sales, marketing and distribution, or manufacturing, production and engineering useful. These offer training in many of the skills that underpin a design career – even though they don't focus on design skills *per se*.

An NVQ can lead to further training at the next level right up to level 5, where you can acquire professional qualifications. If you successfully complete level 3, you could move into higher education in a related vocational area, and study for a Higher National Certificate (HNC), Higher National Diploma (HND) or foundation degree.

HNCs and HNDs

HNCs and HNDs are work-related (vocational) higher education qualifications. While bachelor's degrees tend to focus on gaining knowledge, these courses will give you the skills to put that knowledge to use in a particular job.

Many colleges across the UK offer HNCs and HNDs. In terms of duration:

- an HNC usually takes one year full-time to complete and two years part-time

■ an HND usually takes two years full-time (or longer if you study part-time).

As with NVQs, you may not find a qualification that relates directly to your chosen design discipline, but there are courses that will give you essential skills, such as computing and IT, business and management, and retail and distribution.

HNCs and HNDs can lead straight to a career or you can use them as a basis for gaining professional status. Alternatively, you can convert your HNC or HND to a bachelor's degree; HNCs can allow entry into the second year of a degree, while HNDs can allow entry into the second or third year.

Diplomas of Higher Education

Diplomas of Higher Education are similar to HNDs. They usually take two years to complete and offer subjects such as technology and textile design. You should be able to convert your higher education diploma to a degree with an extra year of study.

Foundation degrees

Many designers in different fields have started out studying for foundation degrees. The qualification is broadly equivalent to the first two years of a bachelor's degree and can prepare you for work or for further study. There are more than 1,700 foundation degree courses on offer (and many more planned), delivered through higher and further education colleges. It takes approximately two years to complete a foundation degree full-time, or three to four years part-time. Most courses combine exams and coursework, plus assessment of your workplace learning. You may also be required to write a dissertation.

What makes these courses popular is that there are no set entry requirements; individual colleges will tell you what they require.

Bachelor's degrees

If you have relevant educational qualifications, you may plan to go to university and study for a bachelor's degree. If you study full-time, a course will take three or four years; increasingly, universities are offering four-year courses that include an element of work experience.

These degree courses are designed to give you a thorough understanding of your chosen subject. There is a bewildering range of courses on offer and each institution's offer will be different to the next, so it's essential that you research the options carefully.

Entry to a degree course is usually dependent upon your academic qualifications, though the demands may be relaxed for mature students. The University and Colleges Admissions Service (UCAS) operates a system called the 'UCAS Tariff'; your previous qualifications can earn points on the tariff to get you a place on a particular higher education course. To find out what is required for a course you're interested in, either read the course prospectus (most are available online) or visit the UCAS website.

Universities such as Middlesex offer foundation courses that bridge the gap between further and higher education in the design field. Because competition for places on degree courses is fierce, many establishments will show preference towards students who have completed relevant foundation courses.

Course info

The intensive Foundation in Art and Design (iFAD) is a unique course, developed to help you progress directly on to an Art and Design undergraduate degree course of your choice at Middlesex University in only 12 weeks. iFAD offers you the opportunity to combine your preparation for a degree course with a gap year: travelling, working and earning to help pay for life at university. Better still, successful completion of iFAD guarantees you a place on the undergraduate subject degree course that you nominate.

(Source: www.mdx.ac.uk)

Postgraduate study

In the academic year 2007–08 more than 8,000 students completed postgraduate courses or study in creative arts and design subjects.

Many designers complete a bachelor's degree in design, then go on to specialise in a particular subject such as interior or textile design. Only you can judge if following a course at this level will enhance your skills and make you more employable – there are arguments both for and against staying on for further study.

There are two kinds of postgraduate course. Taught courses usually take a year's full-time study to complete. Alternatively you can opt for research, which may take longer to complete.

Remember that if you opt for postgraduate study, you'll have to find the means to pay for it. Some funding is available, but it is limited and there is a lot of competition. If you choose to self-finance, you could build up a heavy burden of debt since you may already have student loans to pay off for your first degree.

Your first port of call when you start examining your educational options should be the government website www.direct.gov.uk. Find the section on education and learning. This offers a lot of information and links to other websites that will help you.

To find out about specific courses related to design, the website www. hotcourses.com provides information on hundreds of courses, broken down into individual disciplines and establishments.

CHOOSING A COURSE

Look carefully at different institutions and types of courses before you make a decision. Many colleges and universities hold regular open days, and it's worth going to as many of these as you can. Every department has a unique feel and you need to find the one that appeals to you. Also, it will give you a chance to find out what sort of projects students are working on and whether these have some bearing on your own interests.

According to the Labour Force Survey, just over 40% of designers have a degree or an equivalent qualification. Self-employed designers are slightly more likely to have a degree or equivalent (45%).

The reputation of the college or university you go to can do a lot to get you that first job or freelance opening. Central Saint Martins in London is internationally recognised for its specialist education and research in fine art, fashion and textiles, film, video and photography, graphics and communication design, three-dimensional design, theatre and performance, and interdisciplinary art and design. It offers tuition from practising designers, has a distinguished alumni of top designer names – and attracts talent-spotters who are looking for tomorrow's design stars.

Think about the type of course you want to follow. If you're committed to a particular type of design and you're 100% certain that you want to work in fashion/graphic design/theatre design/exhibition design/interior design, etc., then you can find a course that focuses on your particular preference. If you're less certain about where your strengths and interests lie, consider a broader foundation course that will expose you to a variety of design disciplines.

APPRENTICESHIPS

If you're certain that the academic route into a design career isn't for you, but you haven't got the contacts to find an opening in the industry, you might want to consider an apprenticeship in a relevant career area.

Apprenticeships are open to everyone over 16 years of age, whether they are just leaving school or have been working for years. Apprentices are employees and work alongside experienced staff to gain job-specific skills; with a mentor, they can earn a work-based qualification like an NVQ. At the same time, they study (usually on a day-release basis) for a technical qualification, such as a BTEC, with a local training provider, such as a college. The amount of time spent studying can be anything from 100 to 1,000 hours over the course of an apprenticeship, depending on the sector.

Importantly, apprentices gain key skills that are essential in the workplace, like team-working, problem-solving, IT and communication. And, as you already know, these are valued by employers in the design industry when they are looking for new recruits.

Creative apprenticeships offer opportunities in a range of areas that, although not directly classified as design, could be highly relevant to a design career.

Creative Apprenticeships

From helping to run a record label's office or organising community arts, to managing costumes or running the box office, there are many opportunities. One key area is live events and promotion. Organising events will feed your creative cravings and test your organisational skills; while devising and implementing promotion ideas requires drive and enthusiasm. Community arts workers help many people address social and cultural issues through art. The role is artistic and creative, but involves managerial elements.

There are also more technical roles. Theatre technicians install and operate sound and lighting equipment, while wardrobe technicians organise performers' costumes. Hours are often unsociable, and technical roles can be physically demanding – but very rewarding if you love the arts!

(Source: www.apprenticeships.org.uk)

If you're interested in a career in fashion or textile design, an apprenticeship in textiles is available. Depending on the type of company you work for, this could give you experience as a textile operative working on the production process, or as a textile dyeing technician.

A third area of apprenticeships that could be relevant is IT and telecommunications, particularly if you're thinking of a career in interactive media design.

There are also specific apprenticeships related to computer games development that can help you to become a games tester.

On the commercial side, the apprenticeship in marketing could get you involved in direct marketing (sending a message directly to the customer via mailings, emails or telephone calls), market research (gathering and analysing information on your customers, competitors and the market) and public relations (the public image of your product or organisation). The experience in implementing marketing strategies and plans for

IT Professionals Apprenticeship

On the communication technology pathway of this Apprenticeship you'll learn things like customer care, system security, managing software development, and basic IT applications.

IT professionals serve customers in all types of business. They could be developing software or websites, helping companies set up new systems, or training people to use their IT facilities. On the IT pathway, you'll study software installation, communication skills and technical fault diagnosis, and gain an IT qualification from a recognised group such as Microsoft or CompTIA.

The IT industry is looking for 142,000 new workers over the next three years, so the career prospects are excellent.

(Source: www.apprenticeships.org.uk)

products and services could be invaluable to anyone who is planning to work in graphic or brand design.

SKILLS BASE

One point that has been raised by designers in all disciplines is that design is a business. It relies on developing affordable solutions to clients' problems. As Jonathan Armstead of bluestone design says: 'Design has to be functional and affordable. Developing a successful design business involves balancing creativity and cost so that you achieve a measure of profitability.'

If you want to carve out a successful career in design, creative talent and academic qualifications aren't enough. Whether you work for a large agency or as a freelance, you also need business skills.

> ## One in five design businesses would like to develop their designers' business awareness.
>
> The results are broadly similar by discipline, although there is evidence that skills are most satisfactory in product and industrial design and that lack of business awareness is a particularly common problem in digital and multimedia design.
>
> (Source: Design Council, Design Industry Research, www.designcouncil.org.uk)

Project management skills

At the very least, you should be familiar with the basics of project management. This will help you to understand how a budget will impact on your work, how your time needs to be managed so that you meet relevant deadlines, and how you can work effectively with other people who are involved with a job. Some of this is common sense, but there are particular tools that you can use to help you plan a project, such as Gantt charts and budget sheets.

Before you put your head in your hands because this seems like yet more that you need to learn, bear in mind that many design courses now include a business skills component. This will give you relevant theory and an opportunity to practise business techniques.

Communication skills

Designers, even freelance ones, almost always work as part of a team. They may be involved directly with clients such as marketing managers, or they may liaise with account managers in design companies. Graphic designers may work with copywriters and illustrators; interior designers will commission tradespeople to carry out work; fashion designers will negotiate with suppliers and manufacturers. All of this requires highly developed communication skills so that you can get your message across – and listen to what people are saying to you.

A successful designer is a skilled communicator who can interpret their clients' needs and also communicate their own needs effectively with others.

Presentation skills

Design is a competitive arena and most jobs will involve pitching ideas to clients so that these clients can choose the approach that they want. Pitching ideas and presenting them to clients can be a daunting task – and few novices enter the arena with fully developed presentation skills. If you're going to succeed, you're going to have to work at improving these.

One of the best ways to learn presentation skills is to watch a more experienced colleague. From them you'll learn how to build an initial empathy with a client and get the meeting off to a good start. You'll also learn about the various techniques that can be used to show your ideas. Remember that the ideas should suit the client and their needs. Some people are impressed by all-singing, all-dancing technology and will love your state-of-the-art computer display; others may prefer a simpler, more traditional approach.

Chris Craddock still produces hand-drawn visuals for some jobs:

> *There are only a few 'magic marker' visualisers left now who can draw up a visual design freehand using professional magic markers so that a client can see what the final finished artwork will look like. There's a novelty value attached to these hand-drawn, paper marker visuals. Clients see them as a stepping-stone to the finished item and a great help in presenting ideas to their own clients, whereas Mac outputs containing 'grabbed' images are often seen as the finished item. That takes one element out of the design process, which makes it quicker but can mean that design standards are compromised. The overall design is produced according to what the Mac operator/designer knows he or she can do, so is necessarily more limited and less creative.*

Confidence and creativity

So far we've focused on the practical skills that you need to thrive in a design career. To an extent, these skills can be learned (or certainly improved), a fact that is recognised by the increasing emphasis on business and communication skills in design courses.

Underpinning these, however, are two attributes that you must have before you start out.

- Creative talent – not everyone can be a successful actor, writer, singer or musician. Similarly, not everyone can succeed in design, however committed they are. You have to have a talent for design, a strong visual sense and a real feel for communicating your ideas. This is something that will distinguish you from the thousands of wannabes – and something that you can't learn.

- Confidence – careers in design are immensely satisfying and can be rewarding both materially and emotionally. But make no mistake: this is an immensely competitive field. There are thousands of people competing for a limited number of jobs and commissions. Unless you are very lucky – or have excellent contacts – you are unlikely to walk straight into the door of a major design agency and take your place as their main creative talent. Most designers, in every field, work long hours, don't make vast amounts of money and put up with a high level of job insecurity. They do it because they love the work, and they are confident in their own abilities.

Confidence is essential when it comes to dealing with clients. Yes, you have to fulfil a brief and meet their requirements – but you need the courage of your convictions to tell them what they need and when their ideas are inappropriate. Ian Loseby of Arris says:

> You need the confidence to challenge your clients. If someone tells me that they want a brochure, I'll ask them why. It may be that they end up saying, 'Well I don't really want one, do I?' I'm helping them to solve their problems by working them through. Of course, not all clients are that easy to work with. I can spend all day and night working on something, take it back to the client and they don't like it. When I ask why, they'll tell me they wanted it blue! Do you wonder that a lot of designers get frustrated?

On the plus side, many designers build up enduring, close relationships with their clients. Both Ian Loseby of Arris and Jonathan Armstead of bluestone design point out that with many of their clients there is such a degree of trust that their clients let them make the decisions about what design approaches will work for the organisation. Few professional scenarios are more rewarding than seeing your ideas make a positive contribution to a client's business – and that's what makes design such a satisfying career choice.

⊘ Take action

- Think about the type of course that you want to follow – is it the right level for you? Are you best suited to an academic or vocational course? There are dozens of options available, so you'll have to research them carefully. Look at university and college websites, go to open days, ask for prospectuses, and read all the information carefully.

- Don't think that a degree course automatically guarantees you a job. In the academic year 2007–08, nearly 35,000 students graduated with degrees in creative arts and design subjects and they didn't all find work in their chosen discipline. There are a lot of unemployed design graduates out there, or ones who have gone into unrelated careers. Would you be better combining work in a junior capacity with study?

- Carry out a skills audit and be honest with yourself. Do you have the relevant skills (as well as the creative talent) to succeed? If there are areas in which you think you are lacking, can you identify ways to best utilise your skills? For example, you can learn to make a good presentation – but if you are excessively shy, you're always going to find them difficult and they could make your life a nightmare. Do you, therefore, need to find a design-related career that keeps you out of the public eye?

Chapter Eleven
HOW TO FIND YOUR FIRST ROLE

This is a tough time for new recruits into *all* industries. Whether you're planning a career as a banker or a broadcaster, a dancer or a designer, you'll find that the number of vacancies has shrunk and the number of people chasing these vacancies has grown. So, you can either roll over and admit defeat before you start job-hunting, or you can take a deep breath and prepare to fight for your future. Yes, it is a difficult time in the employment market – but people with talent and dedication will always succeed, regardless of the economic climate.

In this chapter we not only consider the prospects for employment in design, we also consider ways that you can improve your chances of getting that vital first job.

PROSPECTS – WHAT PROSPECTS?

In February 2009, *Design Week* reported that applications for undergraduate design courses had risen by 11.5% since last year, with 40,732 applicants for courses. This increase comes despite warnings from key industry figures that there are not enough design jobs for graduates.

The magazine quoted Ian Cochrane, managing director of management consultancy Ticegroup and former managing director of Fitch and Landor

Europe, who said that design students should 'get out' of a sector that 'does not need you'.

In the same article, John Miller, Director of the School of Design at University College Falmouth, stated:

> I would advise people graduating now to be patient and to hang on to their self-belief. Recession creates churn, and companies which are downsizing now may be losing senior people. When the economy picks up again these companies will be looking to bring in fresh blood… Graduates looking for jobs should also use their time to develop their skills, for example by going on work experience or staying in education. I graduated in the last recession and took a postgraduate course, and when I finished that the economy was in a much better state.
>
> (Design Week, 26 February 2009)

Such comments have to be placed in the context of an economy that is currently experiencing meltdown and a sharp rise in unemployment. *Every* industry is struggling to provide jobs for new graduates. Nobody is finding it easy to get that vital first job. So be realistic about your prospects and above all stay optimistic. If you've got this far – both in reading this book and in your training – you'll find what you're looking for.

GETTING STARTED

There are no rules that determine how you'll find your first job. If you talk to designers in your chosen field, you'll find that many of them have moved into their current roles through a mixture of contacts and luck – they just happened to be in the right place at the right time.

Not every successful designer follows the conventional path of higher education in a relevant discipline followed by a job in an agency. For example, Ian Loseby, who set up brand design company Arris 15 years ago, was studying video and media production at college when he started designing and producing posters for pub events. He didn't make much money – but he did make contacts and quickly realised that he had the potential to develop a business:

I have no qualifications in graphic design. When I was still at college, I started designing posters by cutting up newspapers and sticking letters together, then I moved on to trimming down typesetting books. People came to the pub and said, 'Can you do me some posters for my business?' I was doing paid work, albeit not for a lot of money – and that was a start.

Jonathan Armstead of bluestone also has no formal qualifications and his technical skills are self-taught:

At school the only things I was any good at were sports and illustration. For personal reasons I couldn't go to university and stayed at home. I found a small local design business and went to work for them. I could see opportunities because they weren't communicating well with clients, so I started going out to clients myself. I brought in customers and money and became a partner. I didn't find the lack of formal technical training a problem – if I had a problem, I'd simply look for a solution.

Eileen Driscoll loved needlework, trained in fashion design and now owns a company that dresses film and television sets, and makes leather goods and hats for the armed forces. She joined the company after her hairdresser told her the previous owner needed a dressmaker. 'I couldn't make up my mind whether to take the job or not and tossed a coin to decide.'

Fashion designer Lucy Gledhill also trained in fashion design but worked in retail before a friend of a friend of a friend introduced her to Hooch.

Jonothon Potter completed a four-year design course at Middlesex University, specialising in technical illustration. As part of his course he did a placement at the National Maritime Museum. His work won the Association of Illustrators Best in Show award and this was his starting point for a career that has focused on heritage work and diversified into exhibition design.

However, for every designer who takes an unconventional route into their career, there will be others who follow a path through college or university and then apply for advertised vacancies. So what makes successful candidates stand out when they apply for a job?

Qualifications are important – but prospective employers will be more interested in your portfolio than your academic certificates. It's the portfolio that shows them what you're really capable of and whether you have the freshness and talent that will complement their business.

When Jonathan Armstead recruited a new young designer he had to choose from 50 applicants:

> *Three of them were really exciting, but Richard stood out. He approached tasks in a really fresh way. He took his briefs from tutors and produced very professional pieces whereas many students' work was quite shoddy – they hadn't taken it through to make it look like a finished piece. They hadn't put their all into it – which is what you have to do for your clients. Richard combined talent, creativity and professionalism. He produced a DVD using animation and at first it looked like he'd done everything for the show reel himself, but he was honest enough to admit he didn't do it all himself. That's what we do in the design industry – we use other people's talents when we need them.*

Work experience

When Lucy Gledhill is considering applicants for work experience, she wants to find people who don't already think that they know it all. Yes, she's looking for a freshness and something that stands out – but she also wants recruits who have their feet on the ground and are willing to work within the financial and business restrictions that every design company faces. At the end of the day, a fashion company has to make money or it will go under.

According to the Labour Force Survey statistics published on the Design Council website, 88% of design businesses think that all design students should complete extensive work experience. However, only 54% of design businesses are willing to provide work experience for students. You can do the maths for yourself. The fact is that most employers don't want totally inexperienced recruits – but neither do many of them have the time, resources or inclination to help with the training and work experience process.

> Those [companies] that do not provide placements give a range of reasons for this, the most common being that they do not have enough space or equipment (39%). Another reason for not offering placements is the lack of staff to oversee student work (29%).
>
> (Source: Design Council, Design Industry Research, www.designcouncil.org.uk)

This Catch-22 situation has implications for you when you start out on your career. If you can get a short period of work experience with a design company, take it if you possibly can, even if it is unpaid. This may be a struggle financially but it will pay off in the long run because you'll get essential experience and make contacts.

Beware, however, of unscrupulous companies that are using unpaid labour on a regular basis. In the 'creative industries' a number of employers have realised that they can get staff for nothing by offering 'work experience'. What they actually do is take on a new recruit (without pay) for six months, offer them very little training but use them for low-grade tasks, then, when the six-month period is up, move on to the next recruit. By all means consider working for nothing – but only agree to do so for a few weeks, not a few months – and make sure that there will be a structured approach to your employment there. Ask what areas of the business you will work in and whether you will have a mentor. Make sure that this period will enable you to learn about the business.

If you're at college studying design, your course may include a period of compulsory work experience and your tutors should be able to help you find possible employers. However, there are not always enough places to go round, so you may have to fend for yourself.

If you're looking for graphic, multimedia, product or brand design experience, try approaching companies directly via their office managers or administrators and explain what you want: an opportunity to experience their working environment. Be prepared to talk to a lot of companies before you find an opening – and to do menial work like making the tea and sorting the post. The emphasis for work experience is for you to find out how commercial organisations operate.

Consider working in the voluntary sector if you haven't been able to find an opening with an agency or design company. Charities don't just need sales people for their shops – they also need designers to help with merchandising (useful experience if you're planning on a career in exhibition or fashion design), website designers and graphic designers to help them publicise their work. Offer your services and see what's available.

If you can't get work experience in your chosen design field, look for other employment that is relevant. If you want to go into brand management, look at openings in marketing. If you're planning a career in fashion or interior design, try retailing. Find work that gives you an understanding of what customers want and why they want it. Being able to address problems from the customer's standpoint is invaluable when you start looking for design solutions.

Use your contacts

Any successful designer will tell you that their work is a balance of design and getting out there showing what they can do. Most of them spend more time promoting themselves than in their studios. The same principle applies for new designers who are trying to find their first positions. They have to promote themselves and learn to network.

One of the advantages of following a college or university course in design is that it will help you to make contacts that could lead to employment. Many of the academics who work in the field are still practising designers and they will have their own networks within particular disciplines. They may be able to put you in touch with organisations that can offer work experience or even a job.

Design courses often culminate in displays of students' work that are patronised by talent-spotters. Lucy Gledhill showed her work at the Graduate Fashion Week, which gave her a chance to show off her portfolio and take part in a catwalk show. Rosie Palmer studied Contemporary Crafts at University College Falmouth. She was able to show examples of her ceramics at a show for graduates at the Business Design Centre in Islington.

Don't pass up a chance to show your work, even if it's only on a small local scale. You never know who will see it – and then will want to see you. In the chapter on product design we mentioned two websites, Etsy and Folksy, which offer designers an opportunity to showcase their goods. There are many similar outlets and they are worth exploring.

Finally, let as many people as possible know that you're looking for an opening. It's surprising how many people get their first break through 'a friend of a friend of a friend'. Although there are established protocols for recruiters, many small companies still rely heavily on word-of-mouth recommendations when they're looking for new staff.

Presenting your portfolio

Your portfolio is visible and portable proof of your talent. It also says a lot about your powers of organisation and presentation. A shoddily presented portfolio isn't going to get you anywhere except shown out of the door of a prospective employer.

Think of your portfolio as your first big commercial design challenge. How are you going to make it appeal to your clients? What can you do to help it stand out from the rest?

It doesn't have to be encased in calfskin or decorated with sequins, but your work should be housed in something smart – remember its appearance reflects on your character. So get the best case you can afford and keep it in good condition. Don't get something that is so big you can't transport it comfortably, and avoid stuffing it with everything you've ever produced so that it's too heavy to lift.

Next, think about the contents. Try to include a variety of work that shows different aspects of your talent. Think about the order in which you place items and don't put them together randomly. You wouldn't mix elements such as colour, texture, shape, etc. haphazardly when you were planning a layout for a brochure or a fashion collection, so why would you do it for your portfolio? Find ways to develop an approach in which elements complement each other, or choose a thematic approach.

Think about how people look through books. The final pages often leave a stronger impression than the earlier ones, so you may want to put your most powerful work at the end. Use loose-leaf binders so that your audience can remove pieces they want to examine more closely. You will also be able to rearrange items if you decide that they need a different order for a specific audience.

Ideally, you'll be able to talk through your portfolio with the person who is looking at it – but that doesn't always happen. Make sure items are clearly, but briefly, labelled so that their relevance is clear. Don't be tempted to overelaborate. Potential employers don't have time to read your innermost thoughts that stimulated a particular piece of work. You're supposed to be an expert in visual communications, so let your visuals do most of the work.

Digital portfolios are a great idea – provided that they are a true representation of your work and the person you send them to can open them. Make sure that everything you include on a show reel follows a logical progression and that the whole thing is easy to navigate. If you're a techno-wizard, don't make it too complicated – not everyone shares your passion for technology.

Finally, include a copy of your CV with your portfolio and make sure the whole thing is clearly labelled with your name and address. Sounds like an obvious point, but have you any idea of how many portfolios get lost on public transport or mislaid in employers' offices? Don't run any risks – and, when possible, keep backups of your work.

Preparing your CV

Whether you write off for a job that you've heard about through the grapevine or you apply for an advertised vacancy, you'll probably need to include a CV. Despite the fact that most of us will use CVs frequently throughout our lives, it's surprising how little effort we put into preparing them.

Your CV is one of your most important life documents – it's up there with your academic certificates and the prize that you won for being most outstanding design student of your year. It introduces you to employers and determines whether they want to see you in the flesh and listen to what you have to say. So it deserves attention. This isn't a document you can produce in a spare 10 minutes when you see a job you think you'd like.

There are countless books and training courses that will help you to prepare an effective CV. You can even pay a professional to compile it for you. Many of them will have favoured formats – so don't be surprised if the advice you get is sometimes contradictory.

This book isn't specifically about applying for jobs, so we're not going into any detail about CVs – but we can offer some simple, good advice.

- Tailor your CV to each job you apply for, so that you focus on the strengths and experience that the employer is looking for. You may have to edit it every time you make a new application.

- Keep it short – maximum two pages of A4 paper.

- Start with a brief (four- to six-line) summary of your experience, skills and abilities. Only include information that is relevant to the employer you're writing to. You'll find that summarising yourself in this way is quite tricky – be prepared to write a number of drafts before you get it right.

- List your professional experience in reverse chronological order – most recent first.

- Include a list of key achievements – again, make them relevant to the job you're applying for.

- Include relevant qualifications and training, but avoid wasting space on things that don't contribute to your application. A prospective employer probably doesn't need to know about your Year 6 swimming certificate.

- Include personal information if it is relevant or particularly interesting – it could catch the employer's interest and make them want to know more. Don't bother giving them a list of the clubs you regularly go to on Friday night unless you're planning to work in this particular field!

- Check the CV through at least twice for typos – better still, get someone else to check it. Mistakes suggest a carelessness that could reflect your attitude to work.

■ Look carefully at the design and layout – what does it say about you?

■ Print it out on high-quality white paper. If you're posting it, always send it first class.

■ Never, ever tell lies on your CV. They will come back to haunt you.

As we've already said, there are countless sources of advice for anyone seeking their first job and you should be prepared to follow up some of these. Talk to friends and tutors about how they got their first job. Take advice for every step of the application process – and then find out what works for you.

FINDING THE RIGHT VACANCIES

There are design companies (and advertising, marketing and PR companies that use designers) all over the country, but if you're hoping to get experience with a prestige name, you will probably have to spend some time working in London. Despite a growth in the importance of regional centres such as Leeds, Manchester and Birmingham, the major players tend to base themselves in the capital city.

If you really don't want to move away from your home town, you can still find work – but it may well be with a small agency with a localised client base. Although many of the designers we talked to work outside London, many of them have spent some time there and most of them acknowledge that for ambitious young creatives London is still the centre of the universe.

Before you start looking for a job, you need to make some crucial decisions about:

■ where you want to work – are you willing to go wherever the vacancies are or do you want to stay in a particular location? Getting a fabulous job in London won't necessarily make you happy if you spend most of your time pining for your partner/dog/parents/best friend who lives 200 miles away

- the type of company you'll be most comfortable working in – some people will thrive in a large, cutting-edge organisation; others will find it intimidating. If you're not happy in your professional environment, it will adversely affect your work.

Obviously, we're talking about ideal situations where you have a choice about where you work. In a difficult economic climate when levels of unemployment are high, then that sort of choice may seem to be a luxury as you battle with dozens of other applicants for every vacancy that's advertised. But you should consider these points; you're going to spend a lot of time at work and you need to do everything you can to find the place that will suit you.

Once you've made up your mind what you're looking for, where will you find the vacancies? There are three primary locations.

- the Internet

- the press

- recruitment agencies.

The Internet

The Internet has revolutionised job-seeking. From the recruiter's point of view, it's a relatively cheap way of advertising to a massive, global audience. For the candidate (that's you), it's just so easy. You can apply for vacancies at 3 a.m., wearing your pyjamas and bedsocks. You can compare terms of employment for different jobs, look for vacancies all over the country and overseas, and post your CV so that it's available to anyone who is looking for staff. There's no waiting around for the *Guardian* on a Monday, hanging around in public libraries to get your hands on relevant journals or ringing round agencies. Everything you need is there in front of you, in your own front room.

If you're an interior designer, you can access agencies that specialise in this type of vacancy simply by typing in 'vacancies+interior+designer'. It's as simple as that. Do, however, bear in mind that there are few controls over the information that is posted on the Internet. Anybody can post information – and it's not always accurate. Some recruitment agencies include ads for vacancies that have already been filled because they will attract good-quality applicants. Others are sometimes guilty of hyperbole and oversell the vacancies they have, making them sound much more glamorous than they really are.

The other problem with Internet recruitment is that advertisers may be inundated with applications so you don't hear anything back from them. For your own sanity and safety, follow these guidelines when you job-search via the Internet.

- Keep a careful list of all applications that you submit.

- Print out copies of specific vacancies that you've applied for, date them and, if you don't hear anything within a week, follow them up.

- Call agencies that you've used if you don't get feedback and ask for feedback.

- If a recruitment agency repeatedly ignores your applications, treat it with suspicion. It may not be offering the service it claims.

Although you shouldn't be paranoid, do exercise a degree of caution when you use the Internet. You have no way of knowing who is reading your CV or accessing your portfolio – or what they are doing with the information. Check out an unfamiliar company before you send in too many details about yourself; a quick call to the company should be enough to ascertain that they are who they claim to be and that the vacancies they are advertising are genuine.

The press

Although national press advertisements are expensive, they are still popular with recruiters. The *Guardian* offers the most comprehensive range of vacancies in creative and media in its Monday supplement. If you're planning to go into advertising or marketing, this should be regular reading not only for the job ads but also because it will update you on the industry.

Regional dailies, such as the *Yorkshire Post*, are useful if you're looking for a job outside London. Many smaller companies will use them to advertise for locally based staff.

You should also be reading trade and specialist press for the field in which you hope to work. Design trends change continually and you have to keep up, so you must keep your finger on the pulse, even if you're not working. If the cost of a regular subscription is prohibitive, find out if you can access them via the Internet – or if your local library can get copies for you.

Recruitment agencies

General recruitment agencies can be useful in getting you some basic experience, even if it's not as a designer. Remember what we've said repeatedly in this book: business and commercial experience is useful, so don't turn your nose up at a temporary administrative role in a marketing agency whilst you're looking for that first design job. It will give you useful work experience that you can build on later.

Some recruitment agencies specialise in creative jobs and encourage both Internet and personal applications. It's worth trying to get a face-to-face interview with one of the agents so that you can discuss your prospects. Personal interaction creates a more lasting impression than a telephone conversation or written application.

REMEMBER...

So what do you need to remember when you're looking for that all-important first role in design?

■ Make your portfolio work for you. Potential employers will judge you on it and they need to know that you can deliver the finished goods. Your portfolio should look as professional as possible. Try to achieve a balance of innovative and creative ideas that express your talents with more conventional pieces that a client could use. Remember that design is about meeting clients' needs – and those won't always be for an off-the-wall approach. Don't include half-finished pieces of work, and pay attention to detail.

■ Don't limit yourself by deciding that you will only work in one particular field. You may want to be a graphic designer – but you may find more opportunities in web design if you have the relevant skills. As many of the designers who contributed to this book have

Charles Mitchell, Dean of the Faculty of Arts at the University of Cumbria, says, 'Most people leaving a design course will want to be designers, but the reality is that some won't – they might move into business development, account management and other areas ... However, I would argue that an art school education has a lot more use than just preparing you for a job. It gives you survival skills and an enterprising nature. Designers are survivors – much more so, I would argue, than those who do pure business degrees.'

(Source: *Design Week*, 26 February 2009)

pointed out, design has blurred boundaries and these days it's rare for people to specialise in one narrow field.

- Keep adding to your technical skills and stay abreast of new developments in design software. Most employers will show preference for candidates who can start contributing to the business immediately – they don't have the time or budgets to offer a lot of training. Competence in the main programs that support your type of design is a plus factor.

- Improve your business skills. Many training and educational courses offer business components and these are a great asset to designers. Your work may involve managing budgets and timescales, liaising with in-house and freelance staff, making presentations and negotiating with clients. Proficiency in these skills is almost as important as creativity, and a proven ability to manage is worth a lot to employers.

- Do your research. Before you apply for a job, find out everything you can about the company so that you can tailor your application to their needs. Employers get far more applicants for jobs than they need and the first part of the selection process is to analyse application forms, CVs and covering letters. If you've written something that meets their requirements rather than a lengthy piece about how wonderful you are, you're more likely to get through to the next stage of the recruitment process.

- If you are called for interview, do your homework. You should be informed about the company and the interview process. Think about the questions you may be asked and how you will respond to them before you go. Practise with friends. If you feel really insecure about your ability to present yourself positively at interview, get professional coaching – or at least read some of the books that give advice about interview skills.

Searching for a job is not an easy process. You may be lucky and get the first job you apply for but it's more likely that you'll have to keep on trying. It's easy to become demoralised and to give up. Don't. If you believe in your abilities, somebody else will too. It may take a while, but be persistent – your job is out there waiting for you.

◉ Take action

- Start exploring job search websites on the Internet and look for those that appeal to you. Keep a log of relevant sites, making a note of when you check them for vacancies – you should be revisiting your favourite sites every three or four days.

- Prepare your CV so that you can upload it onto relevant websites or send it out. If you're not confident that it 'sells' you well enough, get professional advice.

- Practise writing covering letters for different jobs.

- Get the *Guardian* every Monday and read through the Creative and Media section.

- Set yourself a target number of applications every week. Don't apply for a job then wait for a result before you apply for another one. You should have three or four applications out with potential employers at any time.

- Don't limit yourself to advertised vacancies – write speculative letters to companies that interest you.

Chapter Twelve
MOVING UP THE CAREER LADDER

Once you have secured a position, how do you go about developing your role and progressing to more senior positions? What is the usual rate of progression from one job to another – two years or ten years? Moving from an in-house team to a design agency and vice versa – how easy is this to do? When should you think about going it alone?

Career prospects vary enormously, depending on factors such as:

■ where you live – if you are tied to a particular area because of family or other commitments, you may find your options are limited, particularly at the beginning of your career. As the statistics show, the majority of large design companies operate in London and the south of England: almost half (47%) of them are based there. So if you're determined to stay in the Shetland Islands, you may find career progression difficult

■ what field you work in – there is more demand for multimedia designers than there is for fashion designers

■ your dedication – as we've said before, design is not a career for wimps. You need to be determined to succeed

■ your degree of flexibility – careers don't always follow a regular, logical path. You have to be willing to take opportunities when they arise, even if they seem to be taking you in a new direction.

Eileen Driscoll now owns a successful company that does a range of work from supplying hats and leatherwork to the Army to helping dress sets on *EastEnders*.

case
STUDY

So how did this graduate of the London College of Fashion develop her varied and lucrative career?

'I loved needlework so I went to the London College of Fashion, where I learned the basic skills that I needed including design, pattern-cutting and dressmaking. My first job was with a costumier and I lasted for half a day – the woman in charge of me was such a bully that I didn't go back after lunch. From there I spent about 18 months pattern-cutting in an East End sweat shop that manufactured clothes for a well-known high-street brand. I heard from a friend that Don Speake and Company were looking for a dressmaker and I got the job. I wasn't sure whether I wanted it – I seem to remember that it was decided by the toss of a coin when I was in the pub with a few friends. It was hard-going at first – as well as working here, I was working in a pub and making curtains to make ends meet. But I loved the work and I was never bored – the job satisfaction made it worthwhile. When Don retired, I bought the company. Although I don't specialise in design any more, I've built up a business that I really love. And if someone wants design advice I can help them – you never lose the basic skills that you acquired when you trained.'

Prospects for career progression are influenced by the nature of the industry. According to research published by the Design Council, the design industry is characterised by very small businesses: 59% of design consultancies employ fewer than five people and a further 23% employ five to ten people.

This is particularly true in interior and exhibition design and in digital and multimedia design, where nine out of ten of all design consultancies in these disciplines have fewer than five employees. Businesses that offer product and industrial design services or communications services, however, tend to be among those with more than 250 employees.

What does this mean for you as an employee? Unless you are working in industrial or engineering design, you'll probably work in a small company and find that your prospects for advancement are limited. You may work your way up the ladder from junior designer to senior creative within the same company, but many new designers find that they have to move companies every two or three years to broaden their experience and find a more senior post.

In a large organisation that has a dedicated design team, or with a large agency, you may find that there is a more structured career progression. If you start as a junior designer you may be able to progress to a more senior position. As your experience increases, you could take on team management responsibilities, and eventually become a studio manager or a creative director.

Don't be afraid to move around if you think that it is necessary to advance your career. The employment market has changed dramatically over the last 30 years and the concept of 'a job for life' is now an anachronism. Whatever career you choose, from accountancy to zoo-keeping, you can expect to change jobs when you want promotion or to gain more experience. Design, particularly, is an area in which mobility is to be anticipated. As we said, in the early stages of your career you may change employers every two or three years. As you become more established, particularly at senior creative or director level, you could stay in one place much longer.

GOING IT ALONE

According to Design Council statistics, there are 47,400 freelance and self-employed designers in the UK. One-third of freelance designers have been in business for less than three years and many of them work across more than one discipline.

A period of economic instability invariably increases the number of people who opt for self-employment, either because they have been made redundant and turn to short-term contract work as freelancers, or because they are new recruits to the industry and find that the supply of first jobs is limited. Then, of course, there are the people who want to work for themselves because they hope it will give them more professional freedom.

Although it may be early in your career to consider self-employment, we've included a section on it because so many designers choose to follow this path.

Many graphic designers choose to work in small partnerships or to go freelance, particularly if they have a secure client base or work in a highly specialised area where they know there will be a steady demand for their work. One of the advantages of this type of design is that you can limit your overheads: as long as you have a good IT system and Internet connections, you can work in a fairly small space – you don't need large offices.

A number of interactive media designers have also found success as freelancers – but there tends to be a greater demand for individuals who are good designers and have technical expertise, so they can do the development as well.

Working for yourself

A day in the life of self-employed Graphic Designer, Conrad Stead

case STUDY

Conrad Stead works as a sole trader (running his own business) and a freelancer (working as a supplier within a larger organisation).

'I didn't think I'd end up as a graphic designer – I bumbled around without much of a career goal, just taking opportunities as they arose. I was always interested in design and what things looked like, and I do have an eye for it, which is key. It's no good being in this job if you can't "see" design, differentiate good design from poor design and if you're not interested in how designs are created or what makes them good.

'I work from home most of the time, so first thing in the morning I look at my diary to see what I have pre-planned and make a "to do" list for the day (handwritten, in fountain pen!). Then I make phone calls, chase up invoices, contact clients and suppliers, go to the bank, buy supplies and get on with the admin and paperwork.

I also try to arrange any meetings for the morning, leaving me the afternoon for longer tasks like inputting and actual design.

'I spend about 25% of my time on admin. On a day-to-day basis that involves preparing quotes and proposals, making phone calls, and chasing up briefs, amendments and invoices. I'm also dealing with clients, on the phone or face to face, which can require a lot of patience. Invoicing and money matters like tax and VAT take up a fair amount of time, and then there's the office to run – even simple tasks like maintaining stationery supplies and the computer system take time.

'When I've finished with all of that, I get down to the design work. I always start by going over what I was doing the previous day, checking and amending, to "warm me up" for the hours ahead.

'If I'm working on more than one job at a time (and I usually am), I will interrupt my work to answer calls, respond to queries and generally be available to clients and colleagues working on the various jobs in progress.

'I don't work 9 to 5. I do my work in about three-hour slots and will keep going until 6 or 7 in the evening – and very occasionally into the night, if I need to. I don't like doing this, as it takes away from my family life – and relaxation!

'I love the variety of the work – there's constant change and you don't get into a rut. Also, this work gives me the opportunity to be creative. I love sitting down at a blank screen and getting my teeth into a piece of design work, finding ways of doing things, solving problems as they arise. It's so satisfying to be able to produce something you know is good – and something that the client likes, too.

'The other plus is being my own boss and not having to work to other people's schedules and structures – apart from my clients', which is different.

'It's not all perfect, though. It's frustrating not being able to do a job because of lack of clarity, when you don't get a proper, clear brief from a client. It rarely happens now as I'm more experienced, but it used to happen a lot, and it can damage your confidence. This is definitely something you can only get from experience. Related to that, another drawback is spending lots of time on a design only to be knocked back by the client and having to start again. I'm pretty good at it now, but there will always be clients with whom I don't "gel", so we are working at cross purposes.

'Business and administration/management skills are very important. If you aren't organised, you can get frustrated and waste time trying to find paperwork or remember things. Everything needs to be written down, especially if you're working on more than one project at once (which you almost always are). Having a system in place is important.'

If you're considering self-employment or starting your own business, contact Business Link to find out about 'Starting Your Own Business' workshops. These are government-funded, so free to participants, and cover the basics about establishing the right sort of business structure, tax, VAT and National Insurance, and business planning.

It's also worth remembering that, although word of mouth is the favourite way for businesses to find designers when they need their services, one in four businesses have used a Business Link for help and advice. Building up a relationship with this organisation could have business benefits in more ways than one.

The pleasure – and the pain

Make no mistake, however: self-employment is one of the most punishing ways you can choose to earn a living. As a freelance, your income will be unpredictable. You'll have periods when you can't meet all your deadlines because there are so many of them and periods when you think you'll never work again because it's so quiet. When you're not designing, you won't be earning; that means you are not generating any income when you are pitching for new business/doing your own admin/sick/on holiday/ taking maternity or paternity leave/watching the World Cup.

If you are a one-man band, you are both managing director and tea person. You can't share the pleasure or the pain of work and there's no one to have water-cooler chats with. For that matter, there probably won't be a water cooler. If you work from home, nobody will believe that you're *really* working; expect requests to walk the dogs, meet the kids after school, get the shopping and stop for a coffee with a bored neighbour.

Worst of all, the period of elation when you land a new commission and know that you'll be able to feed your family and yourself for the next few weeks is followed by long periods when you have to produce the goods…

So why *do* so many people choose to work for themselves? There are a number of reasons. Some will tell you it's because nobody else would employ them, but the truth is that most freelancers thrive on the insecurity. It gives life a certain edge; it may be difficult, it's definitely exhausting, but it's never, ever boring. Every job is different and you move at speed from one project to another.

Above all, as a freelancer you will love the autonomy that you have. You don't have to explain yourself to anyone. When things go well, nobody else can steal your thunder. When they go badly, well – you take the punishment, learn from your mistakes and move on. Nobody can tell you off (except your clients, of course) because you're the boss. Self-employment is totally addictive. And design is one of those portable, skills-based professions that lends itself to going it alone.

Protecting your interests

If you work for yourself, at some point you're going to have to get your head around the complexities of copyright and protecting your designs.

Sometimes people steal design ideas; more frequently, they come up with their own ideas but subconsciously are referring back to something they've already seen. That makes it difficult to guard your ideas from others and make sure that you get the recognition for them. To address this problem, there are complex laws that control the ownership and reproduction (literally 'right to copy') of original work.

Put simply, copyright:

- is granted to creators by law (i.e. if you created something original, the copyright belongs to you)

- comes into operation at the moment of creation and lasts until 70 years after you die

- gives you the exclusive right to authorise reproduction of your work. You'll usually give this authorisation in return for a fee.

If a client commissions you to produce a design for them, you'll usually assign the copyright to the client – in other words, the design then belongs to them.

If you're employed, then copyright of your work will belong to your employer.

Unless you're a lawyer who specialises in this field, it can be a bit of a nightmare, so we strongly advise you to look at the Design and Artists Copyright Society (DACS) website (www.dacs.org.uk). Established in 1984, DACS is the UK's copyright licensing and collection society for visual creators.

As a non-member, you can download free fact sheets about copyright from the website. If you become a member, you can use its advisory service and it will collect royalties every time your work is resold in the UK.

PROFESSIONAL STATUS

Membership of a professional body carries a number of benefits for practitioners in most disciplines. You not only get the letters after your name, you're also signalling that you maintain certain standards and are a reputable representative of your trade. Most importantly, when clients are looking for a designer, many of them will start by referring to professional organisations to find contacts.

Here are some of the major organisations operating in the UK. There are full contact details in Chapter 13.

Chartered Society of Designers

www.csd.org.uk

The Chartered Society of Designers (CSD) gives comprehensive information about the society's role and purpose on its website. It states:

> With over 3,000 members in 34 countries. it is the world's largest chartered body of professional designers and is unique in representing designers in all disciplines. ... The Society is not a 'trade body' or 'association' and membership is only awarded to qualified designers who must also prove their professional capability during an admission assessment. ... The Society exists to promote concern for the sound principles of design in all areas in which design considerations apply, to further design practice and encourage the study of design techniques for the benefit of the community.

To become a member, you'll need a qualification recognised by the Society, normally a degree or postgraduate qualification in a defined design course, plus work experience of at least three years. If you don't have a recognised degree or qualification, you'll need at least five years' work experience.

The CSD actively promotes continuing professional development (CPD) and has formalised its CPD points system to help members identify their training objectives and how they can achieve them. The organisation also offers in-house training for design companies or in-house design teams.

This is a timely move, given that recently *Design Week* and independent research group YouGov discovered in early 2009 that the UK design community is apathetic about boosting its skills. The research questioned 836 people, 50% of whom work in UK design consultancies, 25% lead or work on in-house design teams and 25% are on the client side. Only 8% of those questioned spent £1,000 to £1,500 per head per year on training, while 13% spent £500 to £1,000 per head and 21% say they spend less than £500 per head. Just over half say they devote between one and eight hours a month to training of any sort.

The British Interior Design Association (BIDA)

www.bida.org

BIDA was formed in 2002 through the amalgamation of the Interior Decorators and Designers Association and the UK chapter of the International Interior Design Association. It promotes high standards throughout the profession, and encourages and fosters proven design ability.

There are various levels of membership. Entry is via application and interview and you'll need a minimum of six years' experience in full-time employment in the field of interior design to become a full member. Members and Fellows are entitled to use the suffix 'BIDA' or 'Member, BIDA' or 'Fellow, BIDA' after their name.

You can become an Associate Member after completing either a three-year degree or one-year diploma in interior design, or with a minimum of one year's full-time employment in the field of interior design without any formal qualifications.

Association of Illustrators (AOI)

www.theaoi.com

The AOI is a non-profit-making trade association, established in 1973 to advance and protect illustrators' rights and encourage professional standards. Members consist primarily of freelance illustrators as well as agents, clients, students and lecturers. It offers a range of services to members including portfolio, business and legal advice, seminars and events. It also offers an online portfolio service on a dedicated website featuring more than 10,000 images by 500 artists.

British Interactive Media Association (BIMA)

www.bima.co.uk

This organisation was established in 1984 to promote a wider understanding of the benefits of interactive multimedia to industry, government and education and to provide a forum for the exchange of views among members. Membership is open to organisations and individuals with an interest in multimedia.

D&AD

www.dandad.org

D&AD is an educational charity that represents the global creative, design and advertising communities. Since 1962, D&AD has set industry standards, educated and inspired the next generation and, more recently, has demonstrated the impact of creativity and innovation on enhancing business performance.

Members have access to education opportunities, and can build their own creative networks. The title 'Member' is reserved for creatives who are featured in the prestigious *D&AD Annual*, but there are other categories of membership.

Printmakers' Council

www.printmaker.co.uk

Founded in 1965, this artist-led group aims to promote the use of both traditional and innovating printmaking techniques. It provides information, holds exhibitions and encourages cooperation and exchanges between members and other associations. Membership is open to students as well as practising printmakers.

Textile Institute

www.texi.org

The Textile Institute is a worldwide professional network for people working with fibres and fabrics, clothing and footwear, and interior and technical textiles. The Institute has individual and corporate members in 80 countries. Its aims are to facilitate learning, recognise achievement, reward excellence and disseminate information.

Membership is open to individuals and companies that have an interest in the industry – you don't have to be qualified, although there are different membership grades available to those that seek professional qualifications.

◉ Take action

- ■ Make a list of the journals and websites that publicise vacancies in your particular design discipline and draw up a schedule for consulting these regularly.

- ■ Visit the website of any professional organisations that are relevant to your discipline. Many of them contain useful careers information as well as the latest news and opinions about your design area.

Chapter Thirteen
FURTHER RESOURCES

In this chapter, we include contact details of professional organisations and useful books and publications.

Note that for the following organisations we've included website addresses but not telephone numbers. That's because most initial queries can be answered via their websites and, if you do need to talk to someone in person, you'll find contact numbers there as well.

PROFESSIONAL ORGANISATIONS

Association of Illustrators
2nd Floor, Back Building
150 Curtain Road
London EC2A 3AR
www.theaoi.com

The British Computer Society (BCS)
1st Floor, Block D, North Star House
North Star Avenue
Swindon SN2 1FA
www.bcs.org

The British Display Society (BDS)
12 Cliff Avenue
Chalkwell
Leigh-on-Sea
Essex SS9 1HF
www.britishdisplaysociety.co.uk

British Fashion Council
5 Portland Place
London W1B 1PW
www.londonfashionweek.co.uk

The British Interactive Media Association (BIMA)
Briarlea House
Southend Road
Billericay
Essex CM11 2PR
www.bima.org.uk

The British Interior Design Association (BIDA)
Units 109–111, The Chambers
Chelsea Harbour
London SW10 0XF
www.bida.org

The Chartered Society of Designers (CSD)
1 Cedar Court
Royal Oak Yard
Bermondsey Street
London SE1 3GA
www.csd.org.uk

Crafts Council
44A Pentonville Road
London N1 9BY
www.craftscouncil.org.uk

Creative & Cultural Skills
4th Floor, Lafone House
The Leathermarket
Weston Street

London SE1 3HN
www.ccskills.org.uk

D&AD
9 Graphite Square
Vauxhall Walk
London SE11 5EE
www.dandad.org

Design and Artists Copyright Society (DACS)
33 Great Sutton Street
London EC1V 0DX
www.dacs.org.uk

Design Business Association
35–39 Old Street
London EC1V 9HX
www.dba.org.uk

Design Council
34 Bow Street
London WC2E 7DL
www.design-council.org.uk

The Design Museum
28 Shad Thames
London SE1 2YD
www.designmuseum.org

e-skills UK
1 Castle Lane
London SW1E 6DR
www.e-skills.com

The Institution of Analysts and Programmers
Charles House
36 Culmington Road
London W13 9NH
www.iap.org.uk

Institute of Designers in Ireland
The Digitial Hub
Rose Lane
Thomas Street
Dublin 8
Republic of Ireland
www.idi-design.ie

International Society of Typographic Designers (ISTD)
PO Box 725
Taunton
Somerset TA2 8WE
www.istd.org.uk

The National Society for Education in Art and Design (NSEAD)
The Gatehouse
Corsham Court
Corsham
Wiltshire SN13 0BZ
www.nsead.org

The Textile Institute
Textile Institute Headquarters
1st Floor, St James's Buildings
Oxford Street
Manchester M1 6FQ
www.texi.org

UK Fashion Exports (including the Register of Apparel and Textile Designers)
5 Portland Place
London W1B 1PW
www.ukfashionexports.com

www.thedesigntrust.co.uk
Design-Nation is the new name for The Design Trust. It promotes the
excellence of British design, it manages the Eureka project (which
creates links between designers, retailers and manufacturers) and it helps
designers with business training after they leave college. Over the years
Design-Nation has helped around 1,000 designers establish successful
businesses and currently represents 140 of the most talented designers

working in Britain. The website includes the downloadable 'Business Start-up Guide for Designers and Makers', which is aimed specifically at designers who want to start their own business but find the prospect daunting. It covers the main topics that a fledgling business must address and provides continuous signposting to business support.

www.designnation.co.uk is a major commissioning resource offering direct access to these designers, whose work includes ceramics, glass, furniture, lighting, textiles, silver, metal, jewellery, fashion accessories, branding and product design.

www.skillset.org
Skillset is the Sector Skills Council for Creative Media and works to raise skills levels in every sector of industry within its remit. It subdivides the creative media industries into ten sectors:

- animation
- computer games
- facilities (which includes post-production, studio and equipment hire, special physical effects, outside broadcast, processing laboratories, transmission, manufacture of AV equipment and other services for film and TV)
- film
- interactive media
- other content creation (pop promos, corporate and commercials production)
- photo imaging
- publishing (books, journals, magazines, newspapers, directories and databases, news agencies and electronic information services)
- radio
- television.

Its website carries a lot of useful information about career paths, what particular jobs involve and educational opportunities.
www.ukwda.org

The UK Web Design Association was established in 2001 to encourage and promote industry standards within the British web design and new media sector. The UKWDA is the largest Internet association in Europe and now has 10,883 members, ranging from the self-employed through to international companies from many industry sectors, including publishing, marketing, design, e-commerce, television and education.

CAREERS ADVICE AND RECRUITMENT SITES

www.ideasfactory.com
Ideas Factory has been created with the aims of: helping you make the first – or next – move in your career; aiding you in your creative development; encouraging conversation with other creative people, enabling you to exchange ideas, experience, knowledge and views; opening a doorway into the real world of creativity, arts and media, including through access to insiders' views of what happens in the creative industries; enabling you to get involved in live creative projects and helping you to enjoy creative challenges with a real outcome.

www.design4design.com
Design 4 Design is an online resource centre for architects and designers. The site has all the information you need in one place. Along with the latest news, articles and the best products, choose from sections including: 'Jobs, courses and colleges', 'Products; articles and features' and 'Books and magazines'.

www.creativepool.co.uk
This website offers hundreds of vacancies for designers of all types. You can also upload your CV and portfolio, browse and apply for jobs via the site.

www.careersadvice.direct.gov.uk
Government careers site, useful for up-to-date information about new training and careers initiatives, general information and job search tools.

www.ca.courses-careers.com

Includes sections on higher education and graduate careers, links
to other sites and specific information on careers in different design
disciplines.

www.connexions-direct.com
The 'jobs4u' section is a useful first port of call, and divides careers into
families – there is one on design.

www.canucutit.co.uk
Trendy website about fashion design careers – fun and useful.

INFORMATION ABOUT COURSES

www.ucas.ac.uk
UCAS is the website of the central organisation through which
applications are processed for entry to higher education. It publishes
a book entitled *Progression to Art & Design*, which covers further
education, undergraduate and postgraduate courses. This can be
ordered through the UCAS Distribution Team: PO Box 130, Cheltenham,
Gloucestershire GL52 32F.

www.hotcourses.com
Hotcourses is the UK's largest publisher of retail guides to courses
and colleges. Its website provides information on hundreds of courses,
broken down into individual disciplines and establishments.

www.floodlight.co.uk
Floodlight is a directory of all the part-time and full-time courses run by
public-sector colleges, universities and adult education centres in all
of the London boroughs. They publish two books that are available in
newsagents and bookshops.

BOOKS ABOUT DESIGN

This is a very small selection of books that we like – there are thousands
out there! Many good design books are expensive, so ask your local
library to get them for you.

Fairs, M., 2006, *Twenty-first Century Design*, Carlton Books Ltd.

Hudson, J., 2006, *1000 New Designs and Where to Find Them*, Laurence King Publishers.

Phaedon, 2006, *Phaedon Design Classics*, Phaedon Press.

Polster, B., Neumann, C., Shuter, M., 2006, *The A–Z of Modern Design*, Merrell Publishers Ltd.

Raizman, D., 2004, *History of Modern Design*, Laurence King Publishers.

Slack, L., 2006, *What is Product Design?*, Rotovision.

Woodham, J., 1997, *Twentieth Century Design*, Oxford Paperbacks.

MAGAZINES AND JOURNALS

This is only a small selection of magazines and journals for the design world. Surf the net – W H Smith's website offers a useful list of current publications.

General design

Creative Review
Coverage of advertising, design, film, typography, illustration and new media. The only magazine to keep you up to date with the whole creative industry.
www.creativereview.co.uk

Design Week
Design Week is the magazine of choice for over 35,000 design professionals and those that commission and supply products and services to them. Readers have backgrounds in all the disciplines of commercial design. Coverage includes product design, graphics, retail and commercial interiors, corporate identity, architecture and much more.
www.designweek.co.uk

Guardian
The Monday edition has a creative and media supplement that contains a good jobs section. You should also register with the *Guardian* online job-search facility at www.guardian.co.uk

Wallpaper

Published monthly by IPC Media. Features the latest in design, interiors, fashion, art and lifestyle.
www.wallpaper.com

Interior design

Architectural Design

An international bi-monthly architectural publication.

The Architectural Review

Monthly magazine on architecture and the allied arts.
www.arplus.com

Blueprint

With a 25-year track record as the leading magazine for architecture and design, *Blueprint* is regarded by many around the world as the original design magazine.
www.blueprintmagazine.co.uk

Country Homes and Interiors

Articles on property, country homes and interior design.

House and Garden

Articles on domestic architecture, interior design and furnishing.

Icon

A monthly magazine focusing on inspiring buildings, interiors, furnishings and fittings. It celebrates the design process and the talented designers behind the most innovative work.
www.iconmagazine.co.uk

Graphic and brand design

Campaign

A weekly that covers the whole of the mass communication field, particularly advertising, marketing and the media.

Eye

Eye is the world's most beautiful and collectable graphic design journal, published quarterly for professional designers, students and anyone

interested in critical, informed writing about graphic design and visual culture.
www.eyemagazine.com

Marketing Week
Published weekly and aimed at marketing management, this is a valuable source of brand information.

Fashion design

Drapers Magazine
Founded in 1887, this magazine is aimed at fashion retailers – and anyone who is interested in working in the fashion industry. Check out its sister website, www.drapersonline.com, which has a good jobs section, blogs and a great scandal section called 'Off the Record'!

Multimedia design

3D World
International magazine for 3D artists. Each issue analyses the latest trends in the market, offers artistic and technical advice, product reviews, and behind-the-scenes articles on key projects in the industry. There are tutorials and step-by-step guides covering major 3D software packages, from freeware to professional applications such as 3DS Max, Maya, Cinema 4D, LightWave and Softimage-XSI.
www.3dworldmag.com

Computeractive
Fortnightly magazine that includes product reviews and Internet news.

Computer Arts
Best-selling magazine for digital artists and designers, offering tutorials in every issue, covering everything from manipulating photographs with Photoshop to creating amazing vector illustrations, with Illustrator information about web design, typography, 3D, animation, motion graphics and multimedia, plus reviews of the latest hardware and software releases, creative tips and technical advice, and interviews the leading lights in the design world.
www.computerarts.co.uk

Computer Weekly

Published weekly, featuring articles on IT-related topics for business and industry users.

GamesMaster

Published every four weeks, the UK's longest-running videogames magazine.

Imagine

Europe's number one animation magazine, reporting bi-monthly on all aspects of animation worldwide. It is the most comprehensive resource for information on technology, feature films, television, gaming, 3DS Max, commercials, conferences, events and trends.
www.imagineanimation.net

PC Pro

Published monthly, giving an in-depth look at the industry, comment and news aimed at IT professionals and enthusiasts.

.net

Published monthly, featuring articles and news on the Internet.